English
Year 9
Teaching Guide

Susan Elkin

GALORE PARK

www.galorepark.co.uk

Published by Galore Park Publishing Ltd
19/21 Sayers Lane, Tenterden, Kent TN30 6BW
www.galorepark.co.uk

Text copyright © Susan Elkin Limited 2010

Typography by Typetechnique, London W1
Printed in Great Britain by the MPG Books Group, Bodmin and King's Lynn
ISBN: 978 1 905735 37 2

First published 2010

Details of other Galore Park publications are available at
www.galorepark.co.uk

ISEB Revision Guides, publications and examination papers may also be
obtained from Galore Park.

The publisher is grateful for permission to reproduce the following
extracts:

Guantanamo Boy by Anne Perera, Puffin, 2009; The Other Side of
the Dale by Gervase Phinn, published by Michael Joseph, 1988,
© Gervase Phinn, 1988, reproduced by permission of Penguin Books Ltd.;
from A Short History of Nearly Everything by Bill Bryson, published by
Doubleday. Reprinted by permission of The Random House Group Ltd.

Contents

Running through *English Year 9* and holding it together like a powerful backbone are its 50 or so themed passages – poetry, fiction, drama and non-fiction extracts. They range across five centuries. In many ways English Year 9 is an anthology to use as the teacher chooses. You know your pupils, how to meet their learning needs and realise their potential. There is plenty of scope to pick and mix, dip and dive or do your own thing with these passages as you wish.

On the other hand, if you choose to do it as I would, *English Year 9* becomes a pretty detailed, comprehensive and quite rigorous course for the year. Its aim is to prepare this pivotal age group for GCSE, IGCSE and AS which are just around the academic corner.

What I offer in each chapter is the way I would use this material with a Year 9 class myself – starting with detailed passage-based work and moving on to (usually) thematically related grammar, punctuation, oral, spelling, wider reading and other aspects of this glorious subject of ours.

Passages

I have had a wonderful time selecting these passages which, inevitably, reflect my own reading, interests and taste. They are also the produce of many years of classroom experience humbly learning what works – or can or might work – with teenagers. And never, incidentally, underestimate the impact your own reading and taste can have on your teaching. Your personal passions and enthusiasm can be a powerful way of bringing to life even the most unlikely material for the most cynical pupil.

Of course, when I was choosing passages and linking them under the ten themed chapter headings, there were some which I liked and wanted to use but simply did not have room for. And because reading is a continuous, life-long process there are books I have read since I finished writing *English Year 9* from which I would almost certainly have included extracts had I found them earlier. This guide is a useful opportunity to share some of this extra material with you and I have included additional passages relating to each theme. The best way of using them, I think, is for you to devise tasks appropriate to your pupils or – a good learning tool this – get the pupils themselves to make up questions or invent activities to try out on each other. It is yet another approach to comprehension work.

For the passages in *English Year 9* I have provided suggested writing tasks. Anticipating GCSE and IGCSE, I have not included any of the short-answer questions often associated with comprehension work for younger classes. Rather there are two or three GCSE-style tasks which require a detailed paragraph or two to respond to.

And I cannot stress too strongly that there are, of course, no right and wrong answers in English comprehension work. In this guide, I offer ideas as to what a good answer might include, but that is all any English teacher (or examiner) can do. Pupils have an astonishing ability – it is one of the many things which makes them so stimulating to work with – of often coming up with an original or quirky, but nonetheless valid and reasonable 'answer', that is something the teacher or text book writer has never thought of. We must always leave space for this when we try to frame possible responses to tasks. Creative thinking is a vital part of English teaching and learning.

That is why I would always start with careful reading of the passage together in class, probably more than once. If you read it aloud yourself the first time you can usually find a willing pupil – or share it among several – for a second reading.

The most important part of passage-based learning is discussion – which I would usually reckon to sandwich between the two readings. Ask leading questions. Get them talking and thinking. Keep the discussion focussed but do not be afraid of digressions. As the late Heather Brigstocke, former High Mistress of St Paul's and later Baroness Brigstocke, once pointed out to me: digressions are often the best part of teaching because they spring from what the pupil wants to know and/or is interested in at that moment so the learning is far more likely to stick. Discussion, moreover, is one of the skills assessed for the GCSE oral component so the more the pupils practise the better.

Writing about literature

Many pupils – and certainly those still in Year 9 – find it difficult to write analytically about their reading. They tend to skate superficially over the top and, typically, say very little which is useful. They rarely understand how to home in on the details of the text.

I think there is a very simple reason for this. We learn to write by absorbing the conventions from other people's work. Children quite easily learn to write stories because they are told and read stories from infancy even before they can read them for themselves. They know how stories work. Later, if you want them to write a review of a play you show them a few reviews by professional journalists first. They get used to seeing poems, play scripts, magazine articles and many other forms of text so they have some idea of how to shape their own versions.

Very few pupils in their early teens, however, have ever read any literary criticism. So it is hardly surprising that they cannot write well about their reading.

That is why each chapter of *English Year 9* includes a 'Writing about literature' section. In each case I offer a short, but very detailed, comment on a specific line or two from one of the passages. The aim of this is quite simply to demonstrate how 'lit crit' is done and then to invite pupils to practise their own skills by doing something similar based on a different section of one of the passages. Later in the book I also show how to compare texts. This guide provides a second lit crit example for each chapter and suggests a few more ways in which teachers might use it.

Personal writing

I am not in favour of writing 'frameworks', 'scaffolds', 'skeletons' and so on, of the sort often presented to pupils by text books and/or teachers. Akin to painting by numbers they leech all the creativity out of writing which really does have to start with an author and a blank sheet of paper (or screen). Imposed frameworks pre-suppose that, with minor variations, there is only one way of writing the piece. That is not to say, of course, that I would not encourage a pupil to work out where his or her writing is going and to plan it first – his or her own plan, not a second-hand prop.

But bear in mind that the creative process is a very individual mystery and what works well for one person might not work for another. That is why the 'Writing tip' provided at the end of the 'Personal writing' section in each chapter of *English Year 9* is just that: a tip. It is not a prescription. I would never try to impose a particular way of working on a young person I was asking to write creatively.

Remind/point out to pupils that no two professional authors work in the same way: some (Michael Morpurgo) can write only sitting up in bed, some (me) can work only at a desk with a computer, some work out their writing while, say, walking (Edward Gibbon and Charles Causley) and then just pop it down 'whole' on paper and others (PD James and Bernard Ashley) prefer to write in old fashioned notebooks which they later transcribe. There are probably as many ways of working as there are writers – and that includes children.

All the writing suggestions in *English Year 9* relate to the theme of the chapter they are in and I always include a write-in-any-way-you-like option to keep the writing choices as open as possible. Depending how much time you have available, and how much writing you want your pupils to do, you could let them choose one option from the half dozen or so listed. Or you could narrow the choice down to make sure they tackle different genres of writing or so that you can set more than one writing assignment if you wish.

I have always found that creative writing is better done as part of homework or out-of-class work so that the writer can settle down to it in his or her own way. A busy classroom is not, for most people, the ideal environment for thinking and writing imaginatively.

Word bank

These sections use the preceding passages as a springboard for vocabulary extension. We all absorb (often unwittingly) new words and usages from our reading and we can enhance this process by overtly drawing pupils' attention to words with which they might not be familiar.

I try always to find something interesting or quirky about a word – often its derivation – and then link it with other words related to it. As in mathematics, if pupils can see patterns, relationships and logic it can bring learning to life and make it stick.

The examples I pick in each chapter are fairly random and there are plenty of other words in the passages which you could pick out and use in a similar way – and I make suggestions in this Guide.

Do, however, keep such vocabulary work separate from the initial reading and discussion work on the passages. Nothing turns pupils off a piece of text faster than being forced to go through it line by line glossing every word rather than reading it for impact, overall effect and what it communicates. It matters not a jot if, to begin with, they do not understand every word.

It would be nice to think that by the time pupils reach Year 9 they have mastered spelling. Alas, that is what Samuel Johnson called 'the triumph of hope over experience' and we still have continually to reinforce the rudiments of spelling and to stress why it matters. That is why I have worked in some sort of spelling exercise to each chapter of *English Year 9*. You really do have to keep chipping away at it.

Nuts and bolts

Using the chapter's theme and the passages this section revises and develops knowledge of grammar and punctuation. I work on an assumption that most pupils will, by now, have learned most of it before. I offer, therefore, a fairly brief account of the basics with consolidation tasks by trying to keep the subject as straightforward as possible. I hope these sections will seem fairly fresh and prove a useful starting point if you find yourself having to teach some of these points from scratch in year 9.

Although there are no specific questions or tests on grammar and punctuation in GCSE, IGCSE or at AS and A2 level examinations pupils almost always write better if they have some technical understanding of how the language works. You also need knowledge of grammar to write well about your reading or to comment in depth on what others have written. You cannot, for example, observe that the three violent verbs in a line of poetry suggest ... if you do not understand what a verb is.

Even more succinctly the 'Get it right' part of 'Nuts and bolts' is there to try to help you to iron out common errors. The ones in *English Year 9* represent some of my bugbears. You may wish to add more of your own. As with spelling the teaching and learning has to be ongoing.

More speaking and listening activities

Developing what the late Andrew Wilkinson of the University of East Anglia called 'oracy' is a crucial part of English teaching – and an assessed part of GCSE. So it needs to be built into everything we do in class – which is why much of the initial passage-based work invites oral response and activities. The oral section offers more thematic ideas to develop presentation, drama, reading aloud, role play and other oral skills.

Just for fun

This is, I hope, self-explanatory. Pupils usually enjoy quizzes and puzzles and each of these is designed to use – or extend – knowledge of some aspect of English from vocabulary to literature. Valuable subject matter is presented as a bit of spin-off 'fun' or a game.

The activities make useful fillers to use when some pupils have finished the class work and need something useful to do which does not feel like punishment for working hard. Or you can set them for a lightweight homework – or do them together in the last few minutes of the lesson or on a Friday afternoon. Many of these are easy to replicate – you can make up more or get the pupils to do so.

Wide range reading

Arguably, this is the most important section of *English Year 9*. Reading is quite simply vital. It does more to improve achievement and attainment in (all) school work than any other factor. The more they read the better they do – as the 1993 PISA study of 37 countries definitively found.

But there is much more to reading – books of all sorts – than getting good examination results so that the school rides high in the league tables. It:

- helps you make sense of life
- takes your imagination anywhere – in time or space
- develops your knowledge of human nature
- enhances thinking skills (partly, but not entirely, because it develops vocabulary and expression)
- serendipitously teaches you things by absorption. Hungry readers always have better general knowledge than reluctant ones.

And those few bullet points are not meant to be exhaustive. Most teachers could add many more advantages of reading.

My reading lists link to the theme in each chapter and each include non-fiction as well as fiction along with one or two 'easier' titles aimed at teenagers. So I hope there is something for everyone.

The best way I have found to encourage reading is to role model it. Talk – as eccentrically as you like – about your love of books. Read as many titles on the lists yourself as you can and enthuse about them. Or tell the pupils why a particular title is not your personal 'cup of tea', inviting them to try it for themselves and report back on their views.

Make sure that you allocate some class time each week for independent reading – and read yourself while they do. Show them very clearly that reading is not an activity for children which adults grow out of because they have more important things to do. Nothing is more important than reading – certainly within the English Curriculum and, to a large extent, during life in general.

See my book *Encouraging Reading* (Continuum, 2008) for much more on this.

Extension activities

All teachers need a fund of extension activities and I hope the ones I have suggested in *English Year 9* will help. They come at two levels.

'Moving on' makes some fairly straightforward suggestions for reading, writing and research activities which you might offer to a group of pupils who have finished other work early. Or they would make ideal consolidation homework activities for a whole class, especially you want to develop research skills.

'Ready for a real challenge?' is aimed at the truly exceptional high flier – the pupil who whips through all the rest of the work effortlessly at top speed and is still panting for more or, even the boy or girl who has no need to waste time on some of the more basic tasks earlier in the chapter. By definition, such a pupil will be unusual, but when you do meet him or her you need challenging differentiated tasks. The suggestions in *English Year 9* are very demanding, but I hope interesting and absorbing for any pupil in need of real academic stretch.

Imprisonment is a very useful theme because there is so much material to choose from. That in itself could be a useful starting point for a class discussion: Why has so much been written about the experience of being a prisoner?

Is it because, over the centuries, so many literate, or even well-educated, people have been thrown behind bars (from Walter Raleigh, John Bunyan and Charles I to Jeffrey Archer, Papillon and Terry Waite to name six very different people whose work I did not use in *English Year 9*) that it's hardly surprising that many of them have chosen to write about their experiences?

It is a topic which has long fascinated writers of fiction so there are plenty of stories and novels to choose from, too.

Affinity, from which Passage A is taken, is just one of Sarah Waters's gripping novels – also serialised by ITV in 2008 and now available on DVD. Have any of the pupils seen it?

>> Task 1.1

1. Pupils can, of course, choose anything they wish. In discussion with the class first, before setting them the task of writing their own answers, encourage them to talk about words and phrases. Point out these, for example, if pupils don't spot them:

   - 'the slither of heavy-booted feet' (line 20): the onomatopoeia of 'slither' with all its connotations of slippery lightness next to 'heavy-booted' which sounds as if the men are trudging is mysterious and heightens the sense of anticipation as the narrator (and the women prisoners) imagines what the invisible men might look like. It is an image based entirely on hearing

   - 'clogged with fallen fluid' (line 28): the heavy short-vowelled 'clogged' bluntly suggests blockage and squalor while the alliterative 'fallen fluid' sounds feathery and light until you realise it is unattractively congealed on the sand floor of the kitchen

   - 'solemn as savages' (line 52): a neat and original alliterative simile which suggests that the women are not laughing, smiling or even reacting as they chew their mutton. Are they suffering from what we now call depression? The word 'savages' is carefully chosen for a novel set in Victorian times when it would have been a perfectly acceptable term for native black Africans – of the sort most Britons would only have seen in drawings (or photographs) in the second half of the century. It is a good example of a word used 'in period' and worth pointing out as such.

2. A full answer might include the following points:

   - kitchen shared with men's gaol who collect their food first
   - kitchen smelly and squalid ('dark and clogged' floor)
   - meal is greasy meat soup with potatoes and hard rolls – 'all of it horrible'
   - two prisoners collect the heavy cans of soup and trays of rolls and take it back to others in their 'ward'
   - fish served on Fridays to appease Catholics but Jewish dietary needs ignored.

3. A good answer would notice that the narrator:

    ● is imaginative, visualises the men prisoners she cannot see and knows Christina Rossetti's 1862 poem 'Goblin Market' (line 21)

    ● is sensitive to the smells and squalor of the kitchen

    ● seems surprised that some of the women prisoners still have standards as if they were at home 'daintily sprinkled salt upon them from the boxes on their shelves'

    ● is shocked by, and comments on, the poor quality of the food and the fact that they have only blunt knives so they have to resort to chewing it like 'savages'

    ● speaks quite kindly to the woman 'handling her mutton'

    ● sympathises with the woman who is doubtful about eating her meat because she thinks it might have been deliberately contaminated by male prisoners 'for sport'

    ● is at a loss when the woman repeats herself and just mutters like certain sorts of mental health patient

    ● asks Miss Ridley a reasonable question about Jewesses.

> Passage B is delightfully lyrical and very moving. Do read the rest of *The Evil Cradling* if you haven't already and encourage the pupils to do so, too.

>> Task 1.2

1a. 'dreamy lethargy' suggests, of course, that he is not thinking quite straight or very energetically. It is as if he is half-asleep, in a trance or drunk. He daydreams 'in part contemplation and part worship'. He needs something to focus his mind on and uses the bowl of fruit with its beautiful colours and shapes. He is almost learning to control his imprisonment with his mind.

1b. He is dealing with it by making sure he exercises his mind. He consciously tries to 'find a direction' for his thinking. He thinks a lot about the concept of time and what time means and devises a new way of thinking about it 'a complicated and involved structure which redefines what time is'. That way he feels less despair and can be 'calm and quiet'.

2. A good answer would include some or all of these points:

    ● He is astonished ('My eyes are almost burned') to see the fruit – apricots, oranges, nuts, cherries and a banana – there when he pulls off his blindfold. He doesn't usually get fruit.

    ● He is mesmerised and enraptured by the brightness of the colours – 'a feast of colours' – in contrast to his 'flat filthy palm' 'the filthy floor' and 'the filthy towel'.

    ● The sight, smell and taste when he licks the peel fill him with 'quiet joy'.

    ● He feels 'the world recreated in that broken bowl'.

    ● In a sense he loves the fruit – he strokes it and rearranges it. That is why he cannot eat it.

3. A sensible, thoughtful answer might say that:

- the present tense makes it feel immediate, like a radio broadcast or a diary as if we are there with him rather than reading a retrospective account of something which happened in the past

- it means he can be very direct in addressing the reader/or himself: 'But wait', 'I cannot' and 'I shrug' as if he were speaking rather than writing. It makes it almost conversational although it is of course actually very carefully written

- combined with his frequent use of short, direct sentences such as 'There is silence' and 'I am filled and satiated by it', the present tense works much better here than the past would have done because it makes you privy to his intimate thoughts – now. He could never effectively have conveyed 'They do not confuse me' or 'I am entranced by colour' with the wordiness of the past tense.

>> Task 1.3

Writing text comparisons is quite challenging for most Year 9 pupils but it is required for GCSE, IGCSE, AS and A2 so it is time to begin to master the skills.

Discussion – as Task 1.3 makes clear – is the best way to start. I would begin with the whole group and then, if it's appropriate, set them to pair work as Task 1.3 suggests:

- Do not be afraid of the obvious differences. Start with them. The passage from *Affinity* purports to be written by a prison visitor (who will go home at the end of the day) but Keenan is himself the prisoner.

- Sarah Waters's fictional narrator is writing in Victorian English so it is quite stilted: 'Then the sounds grew less' and 'She said this two or three times'. Keenan's real life first person account is much more passionate: 'I feel the colour in a quiet somnambulant rage'.

- Waters's prison visitor is trying (or pretending) to describe precisely what she saw and heard as if she were writing a report. Keenan is writing very subjectively almost entirely about his own feelings.

- There are similarities too: both passages mention filth and both are about food and reactions to it.

- Both are written in the first person; Waters, unlike Keenan, uses the past tense.

- Keenan is finding imaginative, internal ways of coming to terms with his imprisonment and there's a religious quality in the writing: 'I want to bow down before it'. The narrator of *Affinity* is shocked and puzzled by what she sees – at this stage she takes nothing she sees for granted. There is a freshness and curiosity in her reactions.

Once the pupils have assembled their thoughts and made some notes, encourage them to plan their essay by choosing three or four aspects – such as present tense/past tense or objective/subjective – of the two passages to compare. Limit it or they will get bogged down. Each one of these points can be a paragraph or two in length. The essay also needs an introduction and a conclusion.

Encourage this sort of comparative language:

- Waters writes … Keenan, on the other hand …

- Like Keenan, Waters …

- Both writers …

- While Keenan makes clear …, Waters …

Insist that the comparing and contrasting is threaded through the whole essay. Do not let pupils get into the habit of writing first about one text and then about the other with a comparison (of sorts) tacked on the end. In effect, that is not a comparison at all; it is two mini-essays with a contrived conclusion.

An overall length of 350–500 words is fine at this stage.

Passages C, D and E

I think it makes sense to discuss and study all three of these poems – two from opposite ends of the nineteenth century and one from the mid-seventeenth centrury – before attempting any writing. It gives you the scope to point out overall similarities and differences and to consider three very different poetic techniques. If you prefer, however, there's no reason why you should not take each poem separately and get the pupils to write answers to questions you or they devise.

When I teach poetry I usually tell, or remind, pupils that the Greeks tended to see music and poetry – both inspired by muses – as the same art form. In other words, music has much in common with poetry and is meant to be heard as much as read. In fact, the earliest poetry (Homer's for example) was oral long before it was written. That is why it's important to read poetry aloud, especially in class, and why I encourage pupils to do as much of this as possible and, occasionally to learn some by heart so that they can 'perform' it orally without having to read it at the same time.

With these three poems I would do quite a bit of 'hearing' the verse with pupils before leading them on to discussing it.

>> Task 1.4

1.   A good answer might include these points:

- They were all afraid of death by hanging ('Some prisoner had to swing' and 'Death and Dread and Doom').

- The fear was made worse because they were watched continuously to make sure they didn't take the easy way out and commit suicide ('And by each side a Warder walked/For fear a man might die').

- Their fear was made worse because they tried as a group not to show it as they laboured at the routine prison cleaning, scrubbing, stone breaking, sack stitching and the hard labour ('sweated on the mill') which was part of the punishment.

- The terror which lay still 'in the heart of every man' daily 'crawled like a weed-clogged wave' as it permeated all their thinking.

2a. 'Vile repose' suggests enforced, repugnant inactivity. His 'limbs are bow'd, though not with toil' because the prisoner has nothing to do. His limbs no longer function properly ('a dungeon's spoil') because they have been unused for so long. Originally one of a group of seven 'this wreck is left the last' to age and die in his chains. His agony is made much worse by the loneliness.

b. The two main differences are that the Prison of Chillon is totally, involuntarily inactive while the prisoners in Reading Gaol are kept hard at manual work all day, and that Byron's prisoner is a solitary figure while Wilde's narrator is part of a group.

3. Lovelace thinks he can control his imprisonment by mentally rising above it. His love for Althea with its 'unconfined wings' transcends his being in prison. Freedom to love – both his wife and his king – means that, like the angels, he is free in every sense that matters. 'And in my soul am free,' he writes.

The response to the second part of this question is, of course, wide open and could usefully be discussed at length in a pair or small group before being written up. Of course, you can find similarities as well as differences and they are worth exploring, too. Interesting points of comparison which occur to me include these, but, of course, there are many more:

● Lovelaces's uplifting mental strength is similar in some ways to Brian Keenan's

● The despair expressed in 'The Ballad of Reading Gaol' and 'The Prisoner of Chillon' is very different from Lovelace's positive attitude

● Lovelace doesn't mention (or get bogged down in?) any of the day-to-day minutiae of prison life as all the other passages do. So it's a more spiritual – or even romantic – piece of writing.

4a. It is not difficult to find examples to reinforce the meaning and impact of alliteration whose purpose is often to link words and ideas:

● 'Make a merry masquerade' (Passage C, line 42): is bitterly ironic because it pretends to sound jolly and as if the prisoners are at a dance enjoying themselves but, coming after 'shaven head and feet of lead', it is horrifying.

● 'droop'd and died' (Passage D, line 46): makes an alliterative link between two verbs, both heavy sounding monosyllables which hammer home the awful truth that the prisoner's comrades have simply died around him.

● 'mercy, majesty' (Passage E, line 19): is part of a list of qualities held by the king whom Lovelace (or his narrator) is venerating. The two words have quite different meanings but by putting them side by side Lovelace suggests that they are twin attributes of good kingship. A king must be majestic and distant but he must also show mercy to his subjects as Charles I, for Lovelace, does. Had he used, say, 'kindness', instead of 'mercy' the link would have been weaker.

b. As with alliteration there are plenty of good examples to choose from. In a rhyming poem we unconsciously listen or watch for the next rhyme. Anticipation adds another dimension to our comprehension. Encourage pupils to focus on the effect of end rhyme rather than simply identifying it:

- 'Act' and 'fact' (Passage C, lines 14 and 16): the rhyming words link the coldness of two views of death both of which are in stark contrast to the prisoners' raw fear of it. For the Governor, it's all to do with the law – an act. For the doctor, it's a matter of science – a fact.

- 'eyes' and 'rise' (Passage D, lines 43 and 44): the chiming rhyme of these words reminds us that the prisoner has been denied sight of daylight for more years than he can count. The rhyme heightens the pain.

- 'gates' and 'grates' (Passage E, lines 2 and 4): the hooking together of these words two lines apart connotes the physical boundaries of the prison which are so similar they even sound the same. 'Grates' in the sense here of gratings are the barrier through which his wife comes to speak to him. Gates are what keeps him in prison but he also means the gates of his mind which hold love within him.

C. Internal rhyme adds to the rhythm of a poem as well as to its emotional impact. The pupils will find several to choose from. Here are three to go on with:

- 'grace' and 'place' (Passage C, line 35): the irony of this rhyme is that, despite the linked sounds, there is no grace in this place. It is a 'Murderer's Hole' and there's nothing there to 'help a brother's soul'. The placing of the rhyme reinforces this.

- 'rubbed' and 'scrubbed' (Passage C, line 45): the rhyme of these two words, both of which also have an onomatopoeic quality, evokes the relentless rigorous movement of the prisoners' mops, cloths and brushes.

- 'lie' and 'eye' (Passage E, lines 5 and 6): the rhyme hooks together two aspects of his remembered (imagined?) encounters with Althea when she visits. He feels her hair and he cannot take his eyes off her. The aural effect – with the two long vowel sounds – is very gentle and loving. It is also erotic. Point this out to the class if your think they are ready for it.

5. and **6.** Obviously these questions are open to any answer. If pupils have worked through the previous questions in this task they have effectively made detailed notes which will help them to write their responses to Questions 5 and 6. Encourage them to revisit the work they have already done and, as ever, to maximise the use of 'grafted in' quotes to support their assertions.

Another possible link between passages

I have made it clear in the preamble to Passage C that Oscar Wilde was imprisoned for homosexual offences. This is hard to avoid because pupils are bound to ask why he was sent to prison so *English Year 9* pre-empts that.

I have not, however, mentioned that Sarah Waters is a lesbian or that many of her books feature lesbian relationships. For that reason, she is sometimes shelved in bookshops with 'gay fiction' rather than with mainstream fiction – quite wrongly in my view because her stories are very gripping and she writes beautifully. She is, I contend, a serious novelist and lesbian references are really an irrelevance. Many people evidently agree with me because she is a best-selling author.

Whether you want to point out that this is another link between Passage A and Passage C depends on your own attitude and the maturity of the group you are working with.

If you do decide to explore the topic I think there's a worthwhile discussion to be had about how bookshops and libraries categorise books as well as about to what extent the sexuality of the writer affects our response to his or her work. You might bring in Tchaikovsky's music and Michelangelo's art, too.

Writing about literature and Task 1.5

When pupils try to write about literature, encourage them to use the language of formal grammar wherever it's appropriate – in this example I mention abstract nouns, for instance.

Generally, pupils can see and understand detailed points in discussion. It is writing them which usually presents problems. It can help to train them to jot down phrases during the oral discussion such as 'adamant he will go on praising the king' or 'gentle as well as imperious'.

You can also teach them some lit crit stock phrases such as 'reinforces the main argument of this poem' and show them how to knit short quotations into sentences: 'Linnet-like' he will continue to sing with a 'shriller throat'. Remind them, though, of the importance of quotation marks.

Here is a second piece of lit crit to share with pupils, based on Passage B, lines 12–16:

The first of these two complex sentences is carefully constructed to support the controlled 'calm, disinterested deliberation' which Keenan uses to numb himself from real feeling. There is a strong sense of time, too. It passes very slowly as he has to 'sit again and wait and wait, forever waiting'. The second sentence is also complex but shorter and faster paced. Apart from the word 'always', it relies entirely on plain, monosyllabic words (no longer words from Latin, such as 'disinterested' and 'deliberation' as in the previous sentence) so there's a stark contrast. It also builds up a sense of anticipation because, of course, he has made a mistake. The food is not 'the same as it has always been' and, because of the intensity of the expression, the reader senses that.

Personal writing and Task 1.6

In a sense, it doesn't really matter what sort of creative writing young people do as long as they do some. But if you are going to ask them to write on, say, two of the ideas listed in **Task 1.6**, I would insist that they choose two different genres of writing, such as **3** which invites fiction and **4** which requires a non-fiction response or **5** which asks for informed opinion writing.

Some pupils love writing poetry **6** and that's fine as long as they also write other things.

I think the empathy work required in **2** is probably the most interesting suggestion here; although since Passage B gives us an Irish Catholic being held in the Middle East by Muslim fundamentalists, some teachers may choose to side-step it.

To stimulate other creative writing on this topic use pictures of prisons (such as the one on page 2) and current newspaper articles.

Word bank

A word such as '**somnambulant**' which has such a clear derivation can be an entertaining way into vocabulary work – and an eye opener to pupils who have never done any Latin or Greek. It is such fun for them to learn that funambulism is tight rope walking and that an ambulance was originally a stretcher to carry non-ambulant injured men off battlefields.

'**Necropolis**' (city of the dead or cemetery, from the Greek words for dead and city) is another favourite of mine. It links with words such as necrotic, necrophilia, metropolis. They make good two-minute fillers for the ends of lessons. It is another way of telling stories – often the finest way of making learning stick.

It is useful, too, (Task 1.8) to get pupils into the habit of looking up words in dictionaries. There is no need to be too heavy about this activity though. You could, for example, make it a group activity. Give each pair, say, three words to find meanings for and then feed them back orally to the group. Vary the approach to keep them interested.

> One way of keeping the 'spelling ball' in the air:
>
> Get pupils to number 1–5 on any scrap of paper quickly in the last few minutes of the lesson. Call out five words from Task 1.7 and Task 1.8. Write the correct spellings on the board. Ask who got 5 out of 5 and congratulate them. Tell the rest that you don't want to know about their mistakes but that it is their responsibility to learn the ones they got wrong as a priority before the next lesson.

Nuts and bolts

This section revises the rudiments of sentence structure. It is colour coded and pretty direct, simple and self-explanatory. The idea is to teach (or revise) what a sentence is so that they get the punctuation right – and to help outlaw the all-too-common run-on comma.

Pupils often find it difficult to accept that a sentence can be very short. I often teach this by telling a simple story orally with big pauses and pitch drops at the end of each sentence:

> **Once upon a time there were three bears. They lived in a cottage in a wood. One morning Mother Bear made porridge for breakfast. It was too hot to eat immediately.**
>
> Turn it into a silly game by getting them to clap or stand up whenever there should be a full stop.

Encourage pupils to read their own writing aloud to themselves or a partner in the same exaggerated way so that they can hear where the full stops go.

Another technique is to sit round in a circle and make up a story – one sentence each. The next person takes over when the first speaker reaches a full stop.

Tell pupils that the shortest sentence (and verse, incidentally) in *The Bible* is 'Jesus wept' (St John, Chapter 11, verse 35) and it's a perfectly grammatical sentence with subject and verb. So if they want to write 'Emma laughed' or 'James ran' that's good English. In fact, short pithy sentences are often a sign of good style.

But sentences *never* end in commas.

>> Task 1.10

There is more than one way of creating longer sentences from these short ones – designed to offer practice in constructing grammatically accurate complex sentences and using commas accurately within them. The following are simply examples.

1. Sarah Waters's book, which I have read three times, was published in 1999.

2. Brian Keenan, a university teacher, was held prisoner with journalist John McCarthy.

3 Lord Byron wrote both 'Don Juan' and the long poem 'The Prisoner of Chillon'.

4. Used to being looked after, writer Oscar Wilde spent many hours on the treadmill in prison which broke his health.

5. Most people know little about the life, and only two lines of the poetry, of Richard Lovelace who lived an interesting life in troubled times.

6. Perhaps because it is good at catching criminals, Britain has the highest prison numbers in Europe.

>> Task 1.11

Pupils often have problems with the concept that once you have learned the rules you can break them. But it is what many great writers do. Dickens, for example, uses sentence fragments on almost every page. So, quite calculatedly, do most modern newspaper columnists. Look at examples with pupils to drive home the point – and lead them to notice that good writers usually mix formally correct sentences with other less formal uses – as Keenan does.

The first five sentences are, of course, 'complete'. The group of words beginning 'The shape …' is what computer grammar checkers call a fragment. The sentence 'I want to bow before it' is grammatically 'right'. The rest of the passage is fragmented.

Points to bring out in discussion include:

● It is an attempt at 'stream of consciousness' writing. Keenan wants to convey exactly what came into his mind in the way that it flowed. Most of us do not think in formal sentences.

● Grammatical sentences would have made it stilted. As it is, it is quite poetic – and poems often eschew grammatical sentences. It is also more concise and immediate than it might otherwise have been.

● It is, however, an artificial device. Keenan did not write this while he was a prisoner. He wrote it months after his release, working from memory. He is using a technique to communicate exactly how it was and how he felt.

Get it right

Most English teachers correct this error every day. It is born of the slurring English habit of 'swallowing' the sounds of words which are already elided. We simply do not say what we write – to the bafflement of foreigners who do not recognise 'words' like 'gonna', 'lotta' and 'dunno' from their English lessons.

Well, we are not likely to change the speech patterns of the nation so we simply have to make pupils understand that we have to get these things right in writing and that speech is not always a good guide.

Learning/remembering that 'of' is not a verb might help. You could try getting artistic and/or enthusiastic class members to make a poster saying: 'OF IS NOT A VERB'. Or could someone incorporate it into the desktop of the communal computer?

Jokes can help, too. Present yourself as an eccentric. Write OINAV in the margin of pupils' work. Yelp in mock rage every time anyone gets it wrong. Threaten to tattoo OINAV on their hands. Make them write OINAV at the top of every piece of written work. Be imaginative and find your own quirky way of making them remember it.

>> Task 1.12

This is a reinforcement exercise for spelling, grammar and punctuation. I would let pupils do it independently.

More speaking and listening activities

These suggestions are intended to help you get pupils discussing, reading aloud, improvising role play and making presentations – with a bias towards encouraging them to read around the topic of imprisonment at the same time.

The fourth activity (in the orange speech bubble) is designed to encourage careful listening – a vital but sometimes neglected aspect of oracy.

Just for fun

To prevent pupils writing on their copy of *English Year 9* while trying to solve this puzzle you will need to make a quick copy of the 25 words in the list so they can cross them off as they solve the clues.

Elimination puzzles – and they don't have to be based on book titles – are easy to make up. If they enjoy doing them, get the pupils to make up some for each other. They could use, for example, pairs of words such as step ladder, prison visitor, sitting room, mother board, etc or names of films/TV programmes such as *Doctor Who*, *Blue Peter*, *Midnight Cowboy*. The trick is to pick pairs of words, each of which could be used in a different way in a different pairing – step could also go with mother and prison with board.

Wide range reading

The ten books recommended here range from two very accessible 'children's' novels (but remember that in publishing terms childhood lasts until age 16) to some pretty adult 'big' reads which require reading stamina.

Try reading passages aloud as tasters. **A Long Road to Freedom** is quite episodic and so lends itself well to this. I have read the passage about letters and visitors to Robben Island (Chapter 63, pages 473–478) to classes several times and it has usually inspired some pupils to read the rest of the book independently. And **Great Expectations** is full of wonderful read-aloud passages to use as hooks.

Talk about the books, too. Tell the class about them (expanding on the brief note I provide once you have read them yourself) presenting them as entertainingly as you can.

Watch an extract or two from the televised version of **Fingersmith** in class to get pupil interest.

And add any other books on the theme of imprisonment which you or any pupil has read so that class members can add more titles to their own 'must read' lists.

Additional passage

Khalid is a very ordinary English boy from Rochdale in Lancashire. Then his mildly Muslim parents take the family to visit relatives in Pakistan. Because of a misunderstanding about computer games Khalid is arrested as a terrorist suspect and taken forcibly first to Afghanistan and eventually to Guantanamo Bay, the American prison camp on Cuba. At this point in the story he has just arrived in Afghanistan.

A soldier trips Khalid, crashing him to the concrete floor with a violent yell. A familiar pain rips through his side, giving him the sensation his arms are splintering from their sockets. He bangs his head so hard he blacks out for a second and teeters on the edge of consciousness, coming round only when they start stamping on his aching spine to hold him down before buzzing a metal cutter through the tough handcuffs, allowing his arms to flop to the ground like rags.

Then they begin ripping off his T-shirt and jeans and pull him to his feet totally naked. Surrounding him, one pulls off his hood. Khalid squints at the extraordinary sight of soldiers screaming abuse at naked men lined up against the white walls of a massive hangar-like metal-ceilinged building. The prisoners' heads are bowed in shame like something out of a horror movie as another man photographs each one in turn.

Men with gloves start searching Khalid's body. Touching him all over. Others scream in pain at the intrusive violence of the searches. The worst embarrassment of their lives. Humiliated at every turn by the soldiers' ugly taunts, the naked men are taken to one side and photographed again. When it comes to Khalid's turn, he refuses to move forward. Standing proudly, no matter what they intend doing to him. With a swift punch, he's knocked into line.

Several photos are taken of his face, front on as well as in profile. After that a barber shaves his adolescent face stubble, then his head with the same tenderness as a sheepshearer with a thousand fleeces to go. Then another photo's taken of Khalid with his head shaved.

'OK, move it. You're done!' The photographer dismisses him, swearing harshly at the next man in line to hurry up. The middle-aged soft-faced man, naked, vulnerable, with tears in his eyes, glances at Khalid as if to say the experience means his life is over. It ignites a terrible anger in Khalid, who knows that the shaving of a man's beard – an important part of his Muslim identity – is the final insult for him.

The naked man sits and weeps while his face is being shaved. The barber carries on, while the sight of grown men crying and yelling like babies gnaws at Khalid's heart. The two nearest him, naked as the day they were born, close their eyes and silently pray. It's then that Khalid spots two kids younger than him: one skinny boy about thirteen years old who's acting brain damaged, with his tongue hanging out and his eyes rolling, and another scared-looking boy who's so small he could be eleven or younger. He cranes his neck to see them better, but they disappear from view, when, one by one, men are taken into a nearby concrete building.

Shielded by a soldier on either side, Khalid is shoved into a small room where more American soldiers take his fingerprints, then swab saliva from his mouth before herding him through another door where two men in jeans and white shirts sit behind a green plastic desk.

The biggest American smiles, holding out his hand as if welcoming the shivering naked Khalid to Afghanistan.

'Hi, I'm Anthony. This is Sam. We're CIA.' Khalid doesn't know whether to laugh or cry. Standing there waiting to hear his fate, he's not sure if he's supposed to say hi back to them or not.

From *Guantanamo Boy* by Anne Perera (Puffin, 2009).

Discussion or comprehension points could include:

- the use of present tense
- the use of strong violent vocabulary, e.g. trips, crashing, shoved, punch, screaming abuse, stamping, ripping, etc. Most of these are strong verbs rather than adjectives
- the development of Khalid's character
- the viewpoint: third person narrative but told from Khalid's point of view
- what makes it dramatic?

This topic is another rich seam (to use an apt metaphor) of literary inspiration. As with imprisonment it is worth inviting pupils to think about why.

Interesting to note, too, that not all mining literature is/was written by people like D H Lawrence who grew up with, and in, the industry, although he never worked as a miner himself. Zola, the son of an engineer, became first a clerk and then a journalist. He lived temporarily in a mining community to research *Germinal.* Norman Nicholson and Elsie Balme, whose poems feature in Chapter 2 of *English Year 9,* were outside observers of the effects mining has on a community. It is unlikely that the journalists who wrote Passage C had ever been inside a gold mine.

So, to what extent can you write convincingly about a subject/place of which you have no direct experience? It is another worthwhile starting point for class discussion.

>> Task 2.1

1. A good answer might include these points:

    ● Maheu is working in extremely hot and stuffy conditions. It is 35 degrees and at the top of the space where the men are working there is no movement of air. The heat of his lamp hanging close to his head is making this worse.

    ● Water is dripping onto him from above him. The 'maddening regularity' (line 32) of this is intensely irritating, It also means, combined with his own sweat, that he is very wet, uncomfortable and 'steaming like a wash-tub' (line 34).

    ● He is working stretched out flat in a very narrow space ('like a fly caught between the pages of a book', line 37) which means that his whole body vibrates as he strikes the coal with his pick.

2. This is an opportunity for pupils to be perceptive, even intuitive. They might conclude that Étienne is:

    ● some sort of misfit or a different social class. Why is he addressed as 'the toff' (line 58)?

    ● still learning the job because Catherine is teaching him how to use the shovel (line 59)

    ● not yet good or fast at the job because Zacharie accuses him of laziness (line 62)

    and that Zacharie is:

    ● a risk taker and probably young

    ● laddish enough to have been 'on a spree' (line 52) the day before so he has some sort of hangover

    ● lazy: he stops cutting coal and says he will do some (much easier) timbering instead (line 53)

- a romantic: he starts to dream – perhaps of what had happened the day before (line 54)

- quick to accuse a newcomer of being lazy and to call him names (line 63).

3. A good summary might mention some or all of these:

- the cramped conditions: 'dragging themselves along by their elbows' and 'unable to turn without grazing their shoulders' (lines 14–16)

- the excessive heat and damp: 'heavy air and dripping water' (line 51)

- the way the men have to work one on top of the other lying on narrow planks (lines 1–9)

- the routine that when a piece of coal is cut it falls over the stomachs and thighs of the men at the top before landing on, and being collected from, planks below (lines 23–24)

- the sound: very little talking but the hammering of picks, 'panting breath' and 'groans of discomfort and fatigue' (lines 50–51).

4. This is a pretty open question. I would discuss it at some length with pupils first before inviting them to write an answer. You might draw their attention to:

- The almost scientific detail of the description. Zola tells us exactly how long (4 metres) and how wide (50 cm) the seam is and precisely how the coal is hacked out and collected. It is very graphic.

- The horror of the description which is more effective for being expressed in straightforward language. In order to get at the coal, the miners had to lie on one side with twisted neck, arms above their heads and wield their short-handled picks sideways (lines 16–19). The facts speak for themselves. It doesn't need hyperbole.

- The lack of comment by Zola. He tells us how it is and lets the reader realise for him/herself what the working day is like for these miners.

- The use of occasional short, near monosyllabic sentences. 'Maheu had the worst of it' (line 26); 'Not a word was exchanged' (line 39). These add to the tension and the atmosphere of gruelling hard work.

- Strong images such as 'ghostly forms' (line 45) and 'wild, dirty criminal-looking face' which give the writing immediacy in the style of journalistic reportage.

>> Task 2.2

1. A good answer might notice that:

- Elizabeth is more controlled and quiet although her 'heart halted a moment. Then it surged on again almost suffocating her' (lines 15–16). The old woman's first reaction was to cry 'Oh, my boy, my boy!' (line 20).

- The mother makes a lot of noise and Elizabeth twice tells her to be quiet because she doesn't want the children to be woken up.

- Elizabeth questions the man from the pit while the mother 'moaned softly, rocking herself' (line 23), although she hears the man say that her son had died of suffocation.

- When the older woman wails it seems to help Elizabeth who is 'relieved' (line 34) although she 'wept a little' (line 37) while they waited for the body to be brought home.

- Elizabeth is able to think of practical things, such as how the men are going to manoeuvre a stretcher into the parlour. So she makes the older woman change seats.

2a. A full and detailed answer would probably comment on some or all of the following:

- The rooms: pantry, parlour and the room they're sitting in which has a fire. Both pantry and parlour lead out of the living room. All are small. The older woman has to move seats so that the dead man can be carried in.

- The lack of electric or gas light. Elizabeth goes for another candle.

- The small yard outside the pantry from which three steps lead up to the street.

- The quietness. It is late evening and Elizabeth hears the pit men coming with the stretcher. She hears them before she sees them which heightens the sense of anticipation.

- Lawrence describes almost nothing directly. The details are built into the action. We know there are three steps only because Elizabeth hears the men negotiating them. We know there are two doors into the parlour only because the dead man has to be carried through them. Some teachers call this technique 'showing not telling'.

b. This is a totally open question. Encourage creative answers.

Any pupil who reads the rest of the story will discover that Elizabeth has chrysanthemums growing in her little garden and likes to smell them while she thinks about her, often troubled and less than fulfilled, life. At a deeper level, it is worth pointing out to pupils (after they've come up with their imaginative answers) that chrysanthemums are traditionally and symbolically associated with death in many European cultures. An alert, well-informed reader would guess from the title, therefore, that this story is about death.

3. This is a question which would probably benefit from guided class discussion before pupils try to write anything. Points to draw out include:

- Dialect written phonetically looks off-putting – even irritating – on the page but is usually no problem if it is read aloud.

- It certainly gives a sense of place and reinforces the sense of community amongst the miners and their families. Their common language binds them together.

- Traditionally, dialect speakers were looked down upon as 'vulgar', 'common' or 'ignorant'. Schools insisted that pupils use standard English and tried rigorously to iron out accent and stamp out dialect. Elizabeth, therefore, has probably been to school for longer (or to a different sort of school) than her mother-in-law. There is a sense of educated yearning in Elizabeth – partly evoked by the language of her speech and thoughts – which suggests that she regards herself as a social misfit. D H Lawrence's own mother was rather like this – which pupils may find interesting.

>> Task 2.3

1. A useful summary would mention:

    - the cereal bar and water licked from the rocks which stopped the trapped men dying of dehydration and starvation in the first week

    - the 40 ft pipe inserted by the rescuers through which could be passed food – chicken, cheese, bread rolls, fruit, omelettes and soup

    - the iPods loaded with their favourite music send down to the men on the recommendation of a psychologist

    - the unceasing efforts of the rescuers with low-impact explosives, hydraulic rock-splitters, hand held drills, diamond-tipped chainsaws in hot and difficult conditions

    - Russell and Webb's cheerful sense of humour – asking for unsuitable food and job advertisements.

2. A good answer would mention:

    - lack of any sign the men were alive until thermal imaging detected them five days after the rock fall

    - the need to communicate with the trapped men and get food and other things to them – solved with a 40 ft pipe and a movable tray, like a dumb waiter

    - the impossibility of drilling straight or directly: they had to go 'zigzag fashion' to avoid 'endangering the lives of the men' which would, we infer, have slowed the operation

    - the need to create a metre wide vertical tunnel through which to lift the men out safely. The rescuers did not know whether or not the men were injured

    - the heat

    - the danger of further rock collapses. In the end they had to ask Russell and Webb to spread grout on the rocks around them to hold them together.

3. This is a good opportunity to look in detail at the construction of a (highly) professional newspaper news story – looking ahead to the textual analysis work in GCSE and A2/AS English Language and English Language and Literature. Although it makes Passage C quite a long extract, this is why I chose to reproduce it in full in *English Year 9*. I would always discuss a topic like this and draw observations from Year 9 pupils before asking them to write about it – because they have not yet experienced work of this sort.

    Points to draw their attention to include:

    - The first sentence is a summary of the whole piece. It tells you who (two Tasmanian gold miners), what (rescued) why (trapped for 14 days), where (Tasmania) when (yesterday). You could stop reading at line 6 but still have the essence of what has happened. The rest of the article simply fills in the detail. This is the classic, traditional way of writing a news story. Tell the reader immediately Who? What? Why? Where? When? The opening then becomes, in effect, an expanded headline.

- The second sentence – the rest of the first paragraph (lines 6–10) is there to make the reader feel cheerful and patriotic (if he or she is Australian) or admiring of the Australians if the reader comes from anywhere else. It is repeated later in the article and could very easily be cut here.

- Short sentences such as 'They hugged family and friends before climbing into two ambulances' (lines 19–20) and 'The men were then pulled to safety through a vertical tunnel' (line 42–43) use simple language. They describe plainly what happened.

- Some paragraphs (the ones at line 72 and line 80, for instance) consist of only one sentence. This makes the piece easy to read and direct. It is not a dense, wordy text.

- The facts are revealed in reverse order. The article moves from the rescue and the men's reception at the surface backwards in time to the details of their entrapment and the response of others to their plight – as well as telling the reader about the third man killed instantly by rocks moved by the earthquake. This technique works because a story like this is major news and runs on for days like a serial. Almost everyone reading it would have read most of the background details before so it is revision.

- In a 'good news' story like this, where there is little or no dissent, quotes from politicians and other officials serve to make readers feel a sense of solidarity but they are probably expendable – and appear (if at all) much more briefly in picture-led newspapers which keep their written news items very short.

- The last four paragraphs move on to a wider issue of mine safety – and the coincidental death of one of the journalists covering the story. The news story would work perfectly well without it but – and the *Guardian* is a serious newspaper – clearly there are questions which need to be asked in relation to mining conditions and safety precautions in connection with an incident like this. Many newspapers would run separate features or opinion pieces to highlight these concerns.

>> Task 2.4

1a. Nicholson is comparing the resources being dug out of the earth with the harvesting of currants. Because Cleator Moor yields both coal and ore, it is like finding both black and red currants on one tree. It works (for me, at any rate) because the black currants are black like the coal. The red currants also remind me of droplets of blood although that is simply a personal response and may be off-beam. If you agree with me there are connotations of the physical suffering which is involved in the harvesting, remember there are no rights and wrongs in poetry analysis as long as the text supports it. There is also a reminder that coal and ore, like fruit, are products of nature and that everything ultimately comes from the earth which links with lines 13–16 in which the 'fruit' became too difficult to harvest so it 'lay black and red' left to rot in the deserted mine.

b. The ore of Cleator Moor has been smelted (somewhere) to make steel farming machinery such as ploughs used in Devonshire. It reminds us that the products of mines go far afield. Devonshire is a county associated with agriculture – which gives it a gentle, rural image (although farming is, of course, just another industry and there's aggression in the onomatopoeic 'sliced with the steel') unlike the Cleator Moor area which was highly industrialised. So there's an implied contrast and the suggestion that one cannot exist without the other.

2. The mine re-opens because of a war. Suddenly the pits are 'wick with men' but instead of digging 'For food and life' it is 'the dig for death'. The ore is used to make bullets ('A bullet in a soldier's ear') and the coal is needed to make fire to drive the turbines for armaments production.

3. A good answer might include:

● The mood is wistful ('Of the great mine that was – and is no more'), sad ('Time gone day gone') and romantic ('Sleep soft. South Crofty, pass into dreams, Old Friend').

● The poet wants us to sympathise with 'jobless men' who 'trudge homeward with their fears'.

● She personifies the mine ('Crofty's bled to death') to highlight what for her is tantamount to murder as officials close the mine with 'the scratching of a pen'.

● The comparison of words and rocks at the beginning emphasises how deeply she – like the 'strong grown men' – laments the end of three thousand years of tin mining in Cornwall. She wishes she could, like a miner, dig out more and more words to express her feelings.

4. The poem:

● has 14 lines

● consists of three quatrains and a concluding rhyming couplet as Shakespeare's sonnets do

● rhymes ABABCDCDEFEFGG, also like a Shakespeare sonnet

● uses the iambic pentameter – five strong beats in a line – in common with most (but not all) sonnets; for example: 'So strong grown men might weep to hear the sound'

● is succinctly thoughtful.

How much pupils think this format contributes to what the poem is trying to convey is a matter of personal response but you might point out that:

● Sonnet form enables her to express four separate but linked ideas – wanting to say more, regret for the 'long inheritance,' mourning for the dead mine, an affectionate farewell to it.

● In a sonnet we unconsciously wait for the end couplet to conclude the thought. Like the final chords in a piece of music, we can hear it coming. Elsie Balme uses it very effectively to switch to the second person and address the personified Old Crofty directly.

- The rigidity of format requires her to be very precise and disciplined with words. It could have become forced but it doesn't – the mark of a successful poem.

5. This, of course, is entirely a matter of personal choice. My choice would be:

   - 'Pylons sprouted' (Passage D, line 9) and cross-refer it with 'pylons rusted' (Passage D, line 17) for the poetic patterning and stark contrast.

   - 'Red with the mine's blood' (Passage, E line 9) because I like the image of the mine bleeding away to its death and the fact that the iron pyrites actually turns the river reddish makes it very apt.

   - 'wind that rattles in that empty cage' for its chilling bleakness the stark nouns ('wind' and 'cage') and onomatopoeic verb ('rattles') convey.

   But I'm not a Year 9 pupil…!

6. This is a good opportunity for critical comparison of poetry – but that's quite a tall order for most Year 9 pupils, so encourage preparatory discussion. A good way to start is to get them to identify and list in two columns all the ways in which the poems are (a) similar and (b) different.

Writing about literature and Task 2.5

The object of this is, of course, to show the pupils how to focus on the tiny details in text and to become more aware of how the writer gets effects. As I often tell pupils: written words *never* get on to a page by accident. The writer has selected every word and arranged them exactly as he or she wants. The job of the literary critic – even an embryonic one in Year 9 – is to work out why those choices were made and what effect they have.

> Here is another example of writing about prose, this time based on lines 43–45 of Passage C:
>
> This three-sentence paragraph is pushed into action by the conjunction 'but' with which it starts. The common journalistic technique of starting sentences with conjunctions can be very direct and informal. Here it marks a contrast with the preceding paragraph. The writer has just described the final freeing of the trapped men but all is not happy – a situation summarised by the neatly oxymoronic word 'bittersweet'. The writer highlights the poignancy of Mr Knight's death by qualifying his name with the hyphenated adjectival phrase 'father-of-four'. The use of formal titles here ('Mr Knight' and 'Mr Gill') conveys the journalists' (and their newspaper's) respect for these men.

Another discussion topic

I have referred to the potential political dimension of mining-based fiction in the second extension task (page 40). Some teachers might like to raise it more widely with the class.

Mining literature has traditionally been regarded as left-wing in the sense that it champions the working man and criticises his bosses.

> Typically, mining literature highlights – often with graphic poignancy – the appalling plight and tough working and living conditions of miners. At the same time it usually presents mine owners and managers as – at best – oblivious of the hardships at the coal face or – at worst – ruthless, money-grabbing exploiters of labour. So it's a situation which lends itself to socialist interpretation and story telling.
>
> Is that, however, the only way of telling stories about mining, mines and miners? Would it be possible to tell a plausible and sympathetic story from the point of view of a mine owner or manager? Would any of the pupils care to try?

Personal writing

I think variation in sentence length is one of the most useful things we can teach pupils when we are trying to get them to write better. It really is the difference between 'samey' turgid prose and something which is very readable and pacey. The problem is that pupils are often reluctant to write short, grammatically simple sentences, which they may perceive as childish. So it makes sense to keep showing them examples of real experts using short sentences with elegance, and encouraging them to practise the dramatic three sentence paragraph which I discuss at the top of page 33 of *English Year 9*.

It would be a shame if, having read and studied '**Cleator Moor**' and '**Sonnet for South Crofty**', most pupils weren't inspired at least to try to write some sort of poem – but do stress it need not be about mining. My suggestion of 'something or someone which/who is no longer there' is designed to keep the brief as wide as possible: always a good idea when you are trying to stimulate creative writing.

Because Zola writes so journalistically from Étienne's (third person) point of view in **Germinal** there are good opportunities here for experimenting with journalistic writing and thinking about how it differs from, or can be similar to, fiction.

>> Task 2.7

1. A mural is an art work, usually a painting, applied directly onto a wall.

2. Veracity is truth.

3. Domestic means in connection with a house or home as in domestic work.

4. Extramural study is learning which takes place away from the college or school which organises it. It happens off-site or, literally, outside the college walls.

5. To verify something is to check facts or to establish the truth of something.

6. Transmural is a medical term referring to something such as pressure, which passes through the walls of an organ such as the heart.

7. A domicile is a dwelling place or permanent legal residence.

8. A domain is the land governed by one household or home (or government). It is also used in other contexts such as computing in which a domain name is part of an internet name signifying its home country.

>> Task 2.8

1. Chesterfield: large, tightly stuffed sofa, often upholstered in leather. Straight upholstered arms the same height as the back. Named in the nineteenth century after the Earl of Chesterfield.

2. Tallboy: a high chest of drawers made in two sections one on top of the other. Sometimes called a chest-on-chest.

3. Secretaire: an enclosed writing desk usually with an upper cabinet section.

4. Settle: a wooden bench with a back and arms.

5. Canterbury: a low wooden stand with partitions originally to hold cutlery and plates. Later, often raised on castors, more often used to hold books and magazines.

6. Whatnot: a portable stand with shelves to hold ornaments. Tall, thin and often shaped to fit in a corner.

7. Credenza: a small sideboard, originally one where food was tested for poison before it was served. Sometimes known as a credence table.

8. Davenport: in the UK, a tall, narrow desk with slanted surface and drawers at side. Named after Captain Davenport who commissioned the first ones in the late eighteenth century, probably for use at sea. In America, a davenport is a large sofa, usually convertible to a bed.

>> Task 2.9

1. disappear
2. thermometer
3. incessantly
4. occasionally
5. discernible
6. mahogany
7. collier
8. awkwardly
9. received
10. ploughed
11. psychologist
12. bulletin

>> Task 2.10

These answers are, obviously, just suggestions to give the flavour.

1.   Let's go shopping after lunch. (preposition)

     We'll do the reading now and the discussion after. (adverb)

     He arrived after I had left. (conjunction)

2.   Space travel really took off in the 1960s. (adjective)

     There is too little space in our house. (noun)

     The room will look less bare if we space out the furniture more. (verb)

3.   I am learning to type. (verb)

     What type of bread do you prefer? (noun)

     Some actors quickly become type cast. (adverb)

4.   Alice went through the looking glass. (preposition)

     This is a through train to Edinburgh. (adjective)

     Despite the weak signal I got through to my mother. (adverb)

5.   Did you pass your music exam? (verb)

     The pass rate for music exams in this school is high. (adjective)

     The mountain pass was blocked by snow. (noun)

6.   *Germinal* is the best book I have read this year. (noun)

     You need to book an appointment at the dentists. (verb)

     My uncle is a book fanatic. (adjective)

7.   This game is too easy so let's up the stakes. (verb)

     Do up your shoe laces! (adverb)

     There is a good computer shop up the road. (preposition)

8.   The bowler's got three batsmen out in the first over. (noun)

     That was an argument over nothing. (preposition)

     'Come over for coffee,' said the woman in the house opposite. (adverb)

>> Task 2.11

There is some contentious stuff here so you may find it best to accept alternatives.

1. I would argue – and so does the great linguistics expert Lord (Randolph) Quirk – that these are both possessive pronouns (think of the sentence 'This pen is yours.') but some people regard 'your' in this context as a possessive adjective. 'Mine' is indisputably a possessive pronoun.

2. Is 'off' here an adverb qualifying 'write' or part of the phrasal verb 'to write off'?

3. This is, of course, the definite article but it has an adjectival function in this sentence. It modifies 'fashion' and makes it specific.

4. 'Galloping' here is an adjective qualifying inflation. More specifically it is a gerundive – an adjective formed from a verb.

5. 'Those' is a demonstrative pronoun. It has an adjectival function because it modifies the (plural) noun 'statistics'.

6. As in 1. This, in my book, is a possessive pronoun. But not everyone will agree. English grammar is not a very exact science.

>> Task 2.12

What follows is merely an example of what you or a pupil might make of ridding this passage of redundancy. There is more than one way of doing it. The important thing to get across is that you should try to avoid using two (three or four) words where one will do, Verbosity is never good style. Talk about tautology, too: you don't need 'both agreed' and 'unanimously decided', for example.

> They all agreed on a walking tour around Northumberland, beginning and ending at their Newcastle homes. But they argued about the route. Should they stick to faster tarmac lanes or amble on scenic footpaths? (34 words)

Get it right

I wonder how many times a day teachers and parents correct this tiresome old error in both written and oral work? The trouble is that we see it in print – as though acceptable – far too often these days as in the *Daily Telegraph* example. And that implies a creeping, insidious approval of the wrong use.

So, teach pupils the logic of why Aldrick's sentence is wrong as I set it out on page 37. Getting pupils to learn the examples I give on page 37 and to make up their own (Task 2.13), too – as jokey, as they will – might help. In fact, why not hold a mini-competition to see who can come up with the funniest sentences to show the correct use of 'me' and 'I'? Anything which highlights (and therefore pre-empts) the problem is worth doing.

>> Task 2.14

Using vocabulary in context is probably the best way of learning or consolidating meaning and an exercise like this makes a useful homework. The sentences below are, of course, just examples of illustrative sentences relating to this vocabulary. There are as many possible sentences as there are pupils. Let them use other forms of the words if they need, for instance, to use a different part or tense of a verb or to pluralise a noun.

1. It isn't good manners to flaunt your wealth.

   Rules are there to be kept not flouted.

2. After the accident all the victims were offered help from counsellors.

   Jasper Jones, who was elected last year, is our county councillor.

3. *Germinal* is a fictional account of the French mining industry in the nineteenth century.

   I pretended to have an aunt in Scotland but I'm afraid she is fictitious.

4. I like pop music but am completely uninterested in jazz.

   Mrs Justice Hodgson, who knows the accused socially, could not try the case because she was not disinterested.

5. Paper and envelopes are kept in the stationery cupboard.

   It saves petrol to turn the engine off when the car is stationary.

6. Kenneth Graeme's Mr Toad, who lies so convincingly to everyone, is not exactly presented as a veracious character.

   My brother – who likes no fewer than four eggs for breakfast – has a voracious appetite.

More speaking and listening activities

- The discussion about death is probably the trickiest suggestion here. Omit it, obviously, if you know that anyone in the group is recently bereaved unless you think it could actually help. But you need to be aware and tread sensitively.

- 'Hot seating' – as in the **Germinal** activity – is a useful way both of exploring a literary text and of developing oral skills. If it's successful you could repeat the exercise with one of the women in Passage B.

Just for fun

This is a simple acrostic/anagram puzzle which – for most pupils – will also involve a bit of literary research. Once they have found the titles of some of these books with single word titles, ranging over 156 years, some might feel inspired to try reading some of them. You cannot do too much awareness-raising, however low key.

> If pupils enjoy solving this puzzle, get them to make up similar ones for each other. They could use, for instance, the surnames of writers:
>
> **1.** Black poet whose first name is Benjamin (Zephaniah)
>
> **2.** Author of *Pride and Prejudice* (Austen)
>
> **3.** First name George. Wrote *Animal Farm* (Orwell)
>
> **4.** Novelist and poet from mining area of Nottinghamshire (Lawrence).
>
> **Answer: ZOLA**

Wide range reading

Amongst the seven books listed there are some almost forgotten titles, such as the long out of fashion **How Green Was My Valley** and **Hungry Hill** – both, however, remain as good as they ever were and many teenagers will enjoy them.

Wilbur Smith is a fine story teller whose 'macho' image and action packed narrative might help to hook some of your reluctant boy readers – there is usually no shortage of these in Year 9. Both **Annerton Pit** and **Kit's Wilderness** have boy-appeal too – although I'm not for a moment suggesting that you don't recommend them to girls as well.

Try reading aloud an extract from the early chapters of **Sons and Lovers** to hook them. Lawrence is read much less these days than he used to be but the quality of his writing is astonishing. Try re-reading some yourself if you have forgotten how well he wrote – and then, of course, talk to the pupils about your discoveries. One of the best ways of encouraging and developing reading is to role-model it.

Additional passage

This splendid dialect poem dates from 1906 and 1911 when D H Lawrence was in his early twenties and before he published any of his novels. It needs to be read aloud – ideally with three voices to speak the words of the child, the mother and the caller at the door. If you photocopy it onto sheets (Lawrence's work is long out of copyright) you can work out with the pupils which character speaks which words. Then get them to highlight or underline them in different colours for clarity. Alternatively put the poem on an electronic whiteboard and work out the parts as a group – as I have done it below.

A Collier's Wife

Somebody's knocking at the door
Mother, come down and see.
– I's think it's nobbut a beggar,
Say, I'm busy.

It's not a beggar, mother, – hark
How hard he knocks…
– Eh, tha'rt a mard-'arsed kid,
'E'll gi'e thee socks!

Shout an' ax what 'e wants.
I canna come down
– E says 'Is it Arthur Holliday's?'
Say 'Yes,' tha clown.

'E says, 'Tell your mother as 'er mester's
Got hurt 'i th' pit.'
What – oh my sirs, 'e never says that
That's niver it.

Come out of the way an' let me see,
Eh, there's no peace!
An stop thy scraightin' childt,
Do shut thy face.

'Your mester's 'ad an accident.
An' the're ta'ein 'im I' th' ambulance
To Nottingham,' – Eh dear o' me
If 'e's not a man for mischance!

Wheers he hurt this time, lad?
'I dunna know,
They on'y towd me it wor bad –
It would be so!

Eh, what a man! – an that cobbly road,
They'll jolt him a'most to death,
I'm sure he's in for some trouble
Nigh every time he takes breath.

Out 'o my way, childt – dear 'o me, where
Have I put his clean stockings and shirt;
Goodness knows if they'll be able
To take off his pit dirt.

An' what a moan he'll make – there niver
Was such a man for a fuss
If anything ailed him – at any rate
I shan't have him to nuss.

I do hope it's not very bad!
Eh what a shame it seems
As some should ha'e hardly a mite of trouble
An' others has reams

It's a shame as e' should be knocked about
Like this, I'm sure it is!
He's had twenty accidents if he's had one;
Owt bad and it's his.

There's one thing, we'll have peace for a bit,
Thank heaven for a peaceful house;
An' there's compensation, sin' it's accident,
An' club money – I needn't grouse.

An' a fork and spoon he'll want, an what else;
I s'll never catch that train –
What a traipse it is if a man gets hurt –
I s'd think he'll get right again.

D H Lawrence (1906 and 1911)

On the next page the poem is laid out for group dialogue.

Somebody's knocking at the door
Mother, come down and see.
 – I's think it's nobbut a beggar,
 Say, I'm busy.

It's not a beggar, mother, – hark
How hard he knocks...
 – Eh, tha'rt a mard-'arsed kid,
 'E'll gi'e thee socks!

 Shout an' ax what 'e wants.
 I canna come down
– E says 'Is it Arthur Holliday's?'
 Say 'Yes,' tha clown.

'E says, 'Tell your mother as 'er mester's
Got hurt 'i th' pit.'
 What – oh my sirs, 'e never says that
 That's niver it.

 Come out of the way an' let me see,
 Eh, there's no peace!
 An stop thy scraightin' childt,
 Do shut thy face.

'Your mester's 'ad an accident.
An' the're ta'ein 'im I' th' ambulance
To Nottingham,'
 – Eh dear o' me
 If 'e's not a man for mischance!

 Wheers he hurt this time, lad?
'I dunna know,
They on'y towd me it wor bad –
 It would be so!

 Eh, what a man! – an that cobbly road,
 They'll jolt him a'most to death,
 I'm sure he's in for some trouble
 Nigh every time he takes breath.

 Out 'o my way, childt – dear 'o me, where
 Have I put his clean stockings and shirt;
 Goodness knows if they'll be able
 To take off his pit dirt.

An' what a moan he'll make – there niver
Was such a man for a fuss
If anything ailed him – at any rate
I shan't have him to nuss.

I do hope it's not very bad!
Eh what a shame it seems
As some should ha'e hardly a mite of trouble
An' others has reams

It's a shame as e' should be knocked about
Like this, I'm sure it is!
He's had twenty accidents if he's had one;
Owt bad and it's his.

There's one thing, we'll have peace for a bit,
Thank heaven for a peaceful house;
An' there's compensation, sin' it's accident,
An' club money – I needn't grouse.

An' a fork and spoon he'll want, an what else;
I s'll never catch that train –
What a traipse it is if a man gets hurt –
I s'd think he'll get right again.

Discussion or comprehension points could include:

● Mrs Holliday's character and how the poet presents it – as a near monologue

● the effect of the Nottinghamshire dialect on the success of the poem

● the title and what it tells us about her role in the community

● the part played in this mini-drama by the child

● what this poem has in common with, and how it differs from, Passage B.

Every pupil in the class will have some maritime experience even if they have only gazed at the sea from dry land. And it is a (literally) fathomless subject which has fascinated writers since, and probably before, Homer's 'wine dark' sea and the writer of Jonah in The Bible who tells us that the sea 'wrought and was tempestuous'.

Britons, of course, are more attuned to the sea than some other nations (such as the land-locked Swiss) because we live on islands and none of us are more than 80 miles or so from the sea. It might be worth looking at a map with pupils to reinforce this point. Leamington Spa in Warwickshire is supposed to be the UK's least maritime spot in that it is further from the coast than anywhere else.

Some pupils will be interested in the strong maritime undercurrent (there's an example for a start) in our everyday idiomatic language. Get them to think of examples such as 'all at sea', 'sea change' (from Shakespeare's *The Tempest*, of course), 'ship shape', 'jump ship', 'ships that pass in the night', 'spoil the ship for a ha'porth of tar', 'sail close to the wind', 'take the wind out of someone's sails', 'sail against the wind' and so on.

Talk to them, too, about sea poems they may know but which are not included in *English Year 9*, Chapter 3. I didn't have space for John Masefield's familiar but still beautiful 'Sea Fever', for example.

It might also be an opportunity to discuss island stories and shipwreck fiction as a genre too – from *Robinson Crusoe* and *The Tempest* to *Five go to Kirrin Island* and Victoria Hislop's fascinating 2007 novel about leprosy: *The Island*. 'Airwreck' tales such as *Lord of the Flies* or *Walkabout* are a 20th century take on the same theme, of course.

>> Task 3.1

1. There is no set way of answering this question. Look for two well-constructed sentences which don't waste words but which incorporate some or all of these points:

    ● The sea is rough for several days

    ● The ship is pitching and tossing

    ● There is a lot of noise because items are being thrown about

    ● Most passengers, including the author, are seasick

    ● The crew seem un-fazed.

    For example:

    ● Dickens is experiencing a very rough sea which noisily throws the boat about and dislodges many items on it. Although the narrator, like most other passengers, succumbs to three of four days of severe seasickness the steward and his colleagues seem unaffected because they are working as usual.

2a. 'the domestic noises of the ship' refers to the work relating to feeding the passengers and servicing their cabins. He can hear glass and crockery breaking, as well as barrels and bottles of drink shifting. He can also hear stewards moving about as usual, but falling over.

b. The oblique understatement 'less than exhilarating sounds' means that he can hear others 'too ill to get up for breakfast' loudly vomiting in their cabins or 'state rooms'.

3. His development of the comparison of the wind-tossed ship with, perhaps, an injured, escaped mare includes:

- 'broken knees and failing legs'

- 'stumbling constantly' through 'every variety of hole and pitfall'

- 'a high leap into the air'

- 'a deep dive into the water'

- a somersault

- 'staggering, heaving, wresting, leaping, diving, jumping, pitching, throbbing, rolling and rocking'.

The deliberate overstatement and hyperbole – especially the final manic list of verbs – make it very emphatic and entertaining.

4. Humour is a personal thing. Even if pupils don't personally find this passage witty it's worth discussing why others might. A ten-minute small group discussion would probably help with thought-marshalling before they attempt to write.

Potentially humorous aspects of this passage you might point up include:

- Outrageous metaphors: a ship in a storm is not – literally – in the least like a horse. He compares his shoes with coal barges and the water jug with a dolphin. The effect is very vivacious and indicates that although it was actually probably very unpleasant to be on this ship, with hindsight Dickens is making a funny story out of it. He refuses to take it too seriously.

- The contrast between the very calm steward – which shows that this head wind isn't really much to worry about – and the increasing panic of the author who is joking at his own expense. Worse things happen at sea?

- The initial 'male' pretence that the frightened author is woken only by his wife's 'dismal shriek' rather than hearing, and being disconcerted by the noise himself.

- His final, blunt admission that, of course, like everyone else he was 'excessively seasick'. Throughout the description he's been pretending to be the disinterested observant journalist, wordily above it all. It's a good example of bathos or humorous anticlimax.

>> Task 3.2

1. Facts about flying fish, deducible from the passage, include that they:

    - shoot from the water and are propelled in a straight line until momentum wanes and they fall back into the water

    - swim in shoals – very large numbers visible glittering in sunlight

    - are attracted by light at night

    - often 'fly' snout first into the raft, colliding with structures or people

    - land on the raft, often every night, six or more at a time

    - have red eyes and long breast fins.

    They are useful to the men on Kon-Tiki because:

    - they are easy breakfast – haven't had to be fished for – and taste like young trout

    - they can be used as bait to attract other larger fish for food

    - their shoals are beautiful, 'like a rain of projectiles', to watch.

2. More fish and wildlife seemed to appear (a) as soon as they were alone (presumably there were escort vessels to get them clear of the coast) on the sea and (b) as they got nearer to the equator.

3. Pertinent facts about the blue shark and porpoises that emerge from the passage include:

    - the shark was alone but the porpoises were in a huge, tightly packed school stretching 'as far as we could see from the masthead'

    - the shark is eight foot long and has a white belly

    - porpoises have black backs and 'sprang up here and there all over the sea'

    - both shark and porpoises came close to the raft, perhaps out of curiosity

    - the shark rubbed (scratched?) itself against the stern of the raft

    - the shark – like the porpoises – 'played around for a bit'

    - the shark recognised the threat of the hand harpoon and disappeared (or is that a bit of anthropomorphism?).

>> Task 3.3

1. The statement is, of course, based on an assumption that the reader will know of the Bay of Biscay's reputation for storminess. You may need to discuss this with the pupils. It's a nice bit of quasi-personification too: as if the bay is malevolent, mischievous or, in some way, creating difficult conditions on purpose.

The effects of the bay 'doing its worst' are that the 'grey tumult of water' is, by implication, rough and by the evening of the second day most people aboard the ship are badly seasick, which creates 'fouled cabins and fouler decks'.

2. Before the war, the ship had been a spacious and luxurious cruise liner. E Deck used to house 'the luggage of the rich or food designed for peacetime menus'. The assumption is that it had been requisitioned as a war-time troop carrier before being 'fitted out to take troops'.

3. Points to look for in a good answer include:
   - overcrowding ('crammed humanity')
   - poor ventilation ('the air was bad')
   - sickness made worse by conditions (everyone was sick down there')
   - claustrophobia, heightened by being able to hear screams of panic from lower decks
   - fear of the darkness, disorientation and inability to imagine where they were in thick cloud without moon or stars.

4. There is plenty to say about the description of Sergeant Perkins who:
   - 'came tripping' a verb, which implies cheerful confidence and insensitivity to the feelings of the men who are ill
   - is a 'short compact bodied man', so he's solid rather than fat and looks well when everyone else is feeling very sick
   - has 'bristly carroty hair', which reinforces the faintly unattractive image of no-nonsense everyday fitness in contrast to, say, Rupert Fitch who sits circumspectly singing to himself or Corporal Clark who absents himself from the situation by lying face down with head on arms
   - cultivates a 'belligerent stance' to bolster his authority
   - does not comment – against his own nature – when he sees just how bad things are on E Deck. His reaction underpins the horror of it all. It must have been appalling if it silenced even Sergeant Perkins. The final, simple sentence 'But he was silent' is very telling.

›› Task 3.4

This is a good opportunity to talk about genre – as I hint in the introduction to this task. It is never too soon to draw pupils' attention to the different conventions bound up in different sorts of example – and this chapter provides three cracking prose extracts to discuss.

Having said that, many pupils at Year 9 level find it quite difficult to articulate a disciplined comparison so it's worth stressing (and role modelling) the sort of language which helps (see later in Chapter 3 on page 53 of English Year 9). You – and the pupils – can add other examples of 'comparison language' as it occurs to you. A list might make a useful wall display.

It doesn't matter which two passages they choose, of course. Any one of Passages A, B or C lends itself to detailed comparison with any of the others.

If it helps, encourage them to use the four bullet points I give in Task 3.4 as a checklist or framework for discussion and writing.

I would always insist on a slow, thoughtful re-reading of the two chosen passages before attempting this task.

>> Task 3.5

1. Coleridge's sailors had been chased 'south along' by a 'storm-blast' where they were beset by 'mist and snow' and surrounded by ice which 'cracked and growled and roared and howled'. When the albatross emerges from the fog they see it as a religious portent of better things to come. Suddenly, they manage to break through the ice and a south wind blows them northwards. The albatross is a symbol of hope and they believe that its presence has changed things. That is why they feed and encourage it.

2. Obviously, this is wide open to personal choice. My choice might be:
    - 'as green as emerald' (line 14) because it's such a simple but majestically apt simile to describe an iceberg
    - 'cracked and growled and roared and howled' for its powerful, staccato, onomatopoeic verbs which evoke so vividly the sound of the ice around the ship and the way this is strengthened by the internal rhyming of 'growled and howled'
    - 'in mist or cloud, on mast or shroud' for its careful patterning – the full rhyme of 'cloud' with 'shroud' and the half rhyme of 'mist' and 'mast' hooked together by those four tiny prepositions and conjunctions which give us the driving four-beat, ballad rhythm as the bird perches mysteriously on the ship. 'Shroud' is a deathly word, too, both in its meaning and in its long, mournful diphthong vowel sound.

3. Hatley is 'in one of his melancholy fits' and is distressed by the continued presence of the black albatross. He sees it as 'some ill omen' and, for him, the bad weather the ship has been experiencing seems to confirm that. So he shoots it in the firm hope/belief that there will now be 'a fair wind'.

    Coleridge's albatross seems to be white; most albatrosses are ('alba' means white from Latin). He doesn't tell us it's black and he compares it with a Christian soul. The mariner is therefore less likely to see it as a bad omen. Moreover the helpful south wind blows up before the shooting (not after). So it's difficult to deduce his reasoning from this passage. He clearly feels great remorse and guilt afterwards though. The people listening to his story (lines 39–43) are horrified by what they can see in his face, years later: 'the fiends that plague thee thus'. Perhaps the mariner, like Hatley, is stricken by irrational 'melancholy fits' which we would probably now call 'suffering from depression'. Maybe he feels a sort of jealousy of the happy mariners who believe that the albatross which they're making a pet of ('Come to the mariner's hollo!') has brought luck to the ship.

4. Coleridge:

    - uses ballad form, the traditional way of telling stories in verse. The basic building bricks are four-line verses rhyming ABCB

    - varies ballad form with a six-line verse at lines 5–10 which rhymes AAA BCB which breaks the rhythm and builds intensity

    - uses occasional internal rhyme such as 'fast' and 'blast' (line 9) and 'drifts' and 'clifts' (line 15)

    - matches form to meaning by using all these rhymes, including the 'hiccough' which comes with the double internal rhymes, to convey the manic movement of the ship and the fear that it inspires in the men. The poem rattles along, sometimes bumpily, at great speed – like the ship.

>> Task 3.6

1. This is a useful question just to make sure that they understand the content of the poem. A summary might go something like this:

    - A warship has been sunk by enemy action and a few men are struggling 'like refuse' for survival on the oily surface of the sea. A nearby destroyer throws lifebelts and picks them up. But many men went down with the ship. Cared for and fed aboard the warm destroyer the survivors are outwardly jokey, relaxed and relieved, but inside they are troubled, and later kept awake ('the brain spinning') by remembering the sinking ship and 'the oily dead'.

2a. Ross suggests that people survive through some mysterious determination – 'the casual knack of living' – which those who die don't seem to have. He begins this thought with 'had a mind left for living' to describe the qualities of the survivors. In a sense, it may be literally partly true because some of those who drowned would have given up hope and stopped struggling so, since some of their comrade were rescued, it was lack of willpower which killed them.

 b. 'the oily dead' suggests men who were lost amongst the bits of the ship which sank 'screwing/Oily circles where the hot steel lies'. At another level is the idea that these men were so slippery with such a fragile hold on life that they slid easily into death.

3. Points which pupils might be encouraged to make about 'fingers frozen into claws' include:

    - alliteration and the shivery onomatopoeic effect of the repeated 'f'

    - sibilance of 's' at end of 'fingers' and 'claws' and 'z' in frozen adds to this

    - 'claws' connotes sea creatures, such as crabs, as if the men are ceasing to be human and, as they die, becoming part of the sea

    about 'stupid for a little while':

    - 'stupid' means slow-witted. Only fairly recently has it come to be widely used as light-heartedly silly

- they are acting 'grinning' as if they have learning difficulties – or a mental disability
- 'for a little while' is childish, homely language. It is comforting after the dramatic horror of 'the ship burning in their eyes' and 'the grey ghosts of explosion'

about 'cracked images':

- onomatopoeic violence of 'cracked'
- soft (it's a French word) 'm' and 'ge' sound of 'images' in contrast to 'cracked'
- these are the broken pictures which will haunt the men's nightmares
- gentle memories are now overladen with 'the white faces which float like refuse' and 'the gasping entrance of the sea'.

Writing about literature and Task 3.7

This task is very wide ranging and, I think, as a comparison exercise, it is best done orally. You, the teacher, can then circulate and contribute or make suggestions. The chances are that no two pairs will be comparing the same passage with the Shakespeare if you give them free rein.

It concentrates the mind and helps to keep discussion on track, I find, if you build in summarising your (the pupils') considered views to present to another pair at the end. It also certainly helps to consolidate the learning.

There is no reason why you shouldn't then ask them to write up their views in whatever form you or they choose if you want a written record: notes, two columns, essay, script for a school assembly or whatever.

My exemplar passage in Writing about literature (page 53) might make a starting point because it examines two lines of the Shakespeare.

Personal writing

Writing book reviews is a very specific skill. Teachers often ask pupils to do it and pupils are, on the whole, pretty weak at it. You know the sort of thing. 'I loved this book and would give it ten stars.' Somehow, to cultivate the book reviewing knack, you have to coax them to write much more precisely about what they've read without giving away the entire plot or summarising every aspect if it's non-fiction. The function of a review is to give the review reader enough flavour of the book so that he/she can decide whether or not to read it. The usual vague teenage stuff fails at the first hurdle.

All major newspapers (especially at weekends) carry a number of well-written book reviews. And in most there is also a regular review of a 'children's' (that is up to age 16) book. Make sure that your pupils see, read and discuss a selection of these regularly if you want them to write decent reviews. Remember too how interesting it always is to read someone else's (professional) review of a book you have already read and perhaps reviewed.

Otherwise, there are some quite challenging – and, I hope, suitably interesting – ideas for writing on sea-related topics in this section, inspired by the passages. As ever, keep the choices and opportunities as wide as possible but make sure that each pupil also experiments with a range of genres.

>> Task 3.9

There is some nice sea-linked (or watery) vocabulary here. You could, if you wish, extend it with words derived from the Latin adjective *nautilus* (of a sailor) and words such as 'nautical' and 'nautiloid'. Or consider the words we get from the Ancient Greek word for the sea: *pelagos* (archipelago, pelargic, pelagian). And what about all those words for sailor: seafarer, mariner, boatman, hand, tar and so on. Where do they all come from?

Of course pupils will devise their own sentences. These are just examples:

1. Aquatic mammals, such as porpoises and whales, give birth underwater.

2. Perhaps because it is on the coast, Southampton University is a popular place to study marine biology.

3. The River Thames is navigable to small craft up to, and beyond, Oxford.

4. Aquasports, such as surfing, are tremendously popular in Australia.

5. Navicular plant troughs are popular in coastal towns because they remind people of the boats they resemble.

6. My great uncle, a naval officer in the Second World War, was shipwrecked in the Mediterranean with some of his men.

7. The Romans built an aqueduct across the Gard valley near Nîmes in the south of France to carry water to the city.

8. The marigram indicated that an exceptionally high tide was due that evening.

9. Professor Elwyn Evans, the aquarist who made some TV programmes about marine life, has been appointed curator of the new aquarium in our town.

10. The sea blue-green stone in my mother's aquamarine ring was left to her by her grandmother.

>> Task 3.10

1. Aquaphobia: fear of water and/or drowning

2. Arachnophobia: fear of spiders

3. Xenophobia: fear of foreigners or strangers

4. Agoraphobia: fear of open spaces or going outdoors

5. Technophobia: fear of technology, especially computers

>> Task 3.11

I think prepared dictation is a seriously underrated – and very useful – way of learning spellings in context. If you use a well-written passage it can also help to reinforce the conventions of grammar and punctuation. Sadly, however, it has gone out of fashion and is not much used in modern classrooms. So let's bring it back.

There's no need to be 'heavy' about it. Pairs of pupils can work on a dictation passage together, as I suggest in Task 3.11. That way there's also some inbuilt oral practice because the 'dictator' obviously needs to articulate very clearly. Or, if you prefer and/or wish to be more formal, you could set the learning as a homework and then dictate it yourself as a whole class test.

>> Task 3.12

In my experience, many pupils find the concept of active and passive voice quite difficult, perhaps because most do no Latin these days. And yet, as I explain on page 56 of *English Year 9*, it is actually quite straightforward. It is also very important (a) because it makes such a difference to the tone of a piece of writing and (b) because critical readers and listeners should be trained to spot very easily any writer or speaker (such as a wily politician) who is hiding behind the passive voice.

There is more than one way of 'reversing' some of these sentences especially active to passive (numbers 6–10). Regard the following as mere examples:

1. The cat saw the dog.

2. Everyone enjoyed the meal.

3. *The Times* reported that crime figures had risen.

4. Crowds filled the streets.

5. Jessica Jones played the accompaniment in the Beethoven piece.

6. The cinema is liked by most people.

7. In 1946 a raft was built by Thor Heyerdahl.

8. The Nobel Prize for Literature was won by Doris Lessing.

9. Money is said by some to be the root of all evil.

10. Lyrical Ballads was published at the end of the eighteenth century by Coleridge and Wordsworth.

>> Task 3.13

This is another old chestnut which most writers and speakers get wrong most of the time. I think they quite often do it deliberately because there's a perception that correct placement sounds stilted. But the positioning of these adverbs affects and reflects accuracy and precision (or lack of them) so I think it's worth working at:

1. Marissa was just waiting. (She was doing nothing else, such as reading.)

2. Just Marissa was waiting. (She was alone.)

3. Even George enjoyed the film. (Surprise implied because he's hard to please.)

4. George even enjoyed the film. (He also enjoyed everything else that day.)

5. George enjoyed even the film. (Ditto – interesting because here the position of 'only' doesn't change the meaning. It is the same as 4.)

6. Only my family booked the flight. (Other families made different arrangements.)

7. My family booked the flight only. (They didn't also book, for example, a hotel or hire car.)

8. My family only booked the flight. (They didn't do anything else to, or with, it such as catch the plane.)

More speaking and listening activities

Two of these suggestions focus on '**The Rime of the Ancient Mariner**' for which I make no apology. It is a wonderful poem which probably really does justify the 'seminal text' label and the more I look at it the more I marvel at it even after all these years. (I think I first read it in what we now call Year 7.) Anything which gets pupils to read closely and discuss Coleridge's masterpiece is, in my view, a good thing.

Speaking and listening is also usually yet another research opportunity. You cannot give an authoritative talk about a shipwreck unless you've amassed some facts. They might, incidentally, find James Cameron's 1997 film ***Titanic*** a useful source of information, provided they are clear about which aspects of the film are fictional. And there are some chilling eye-witness accounts relating to the Titanic in **The Faber Book of Reportage** (John Carey [ed.], 1987).

Inventing a shipwreck story can be great fun, too, because there are so many ways you could do it. At its worst, the shipwreck subject (remember the *Herald of Free Enterprise*) is tragic, almost beyond imagining. On the other hand, you could contrive an upbeat (and unlikely) '***Desert Island Discs***' situation.

Just for fun

Word wheels help with spelling and I think they develop concentration and thinking skills. Moreover, most young people enjoy them.

They are also extremely easy to make up. Simply start with a 7, 8, 9, 10 or 11 letter word. Jumble the letters. Put one (choose this with care) at the centre and the others round the edge. Hey Presto! Now give it to someone else to solve. Or collect them from newspapers. Look for 'Target' in the *Daily Express* or 'Polygon' in *The Times*, for example.

I have often set pupils to do this in pairs – each devising a word wheel for the other – for ten minutes at the end of a lesson if, for some other reason, I need a lightweight 'filler'.

The more letters there are in the base word the harder it will be to spot although more letters means more combinations for short words.

Wide range reading

The list speaks for itself although there's so much sea-related literature that you and the pupils can almost certainly add more titles of your own. Bernard Cornwell's **Sharpe** novels, for example, and other novels by Conrad. Do not forget C S Forrester's **Hornblower** books either. Or many will know Michael Morpurgo's **Kensuke's Kingdom**.

Novels with a sea theme, aimed at young readers which I have read since the completion of *English Year 9* include:

- **Forbidden Island** by Malcolm Rose (Usborne, 2009). A rather sinister take on a group of twenty-first century youngsters finding an unknown island. Think Second World War and anthrax.
- **Black Heart of Jamaica** by Julia Golding (Egmont, 2008). Part of a series about the feisty, late eighteenth century Cat Royal. This story takes her across the Atlantic to the Caribbean.
- **Between Two Seas** by Marie-Louise Jensen (Oxford, 2008). Story of a nineteenth century, Grimsby-born orphaned lass who crosses the North Sea in search of her – very maritime – Norwegian heritage.

Additional passage

Henry Fielding (1707–1754) was a novelist, journalist and lawyer. It is worth making Year 9 pupils aware of Fielding, author of Tom Jones *and* Joseph Andrews *since he was effectively the first 'modern' novelist – writing about the scrapes, adventures and shortcomings of fairly ordinary people – whose works led straight to Thackeray and Dickens. In 1754, when he was already quite ill, he set off for Portugal with his wife and one of his daughters where he died the following year. This passage, dated 11 July 1754, comes from the posthumously published account he wrote of the journey.*

A most tragical incident fell out this day at sea. While the ship was under sail, but making as will appear no great way, a kitten, one of four of the feline inhabitants of the cabin, fell from the window into the water: an alarm was immediately given to the captain, who was then upon deck, and received it with utmost concern and many bitter oaths. He immediately gave orders to the steersman in favour of the poor thing, as he called it; the sails were instantly slackened, and all hands, as the phrase is, employed to recover the poor animal. I was, I own, extremely surprised at all this; less indeed at the captain's extreme tenderness than at his conceiving any possibility of success; for if puss had had nine thousand instead of nine lives, I concluded they had all been lost. The boatswain, however, had more sanguine hopes, for, having stripped himself of his jacket, breeches and shirt, he leaped boldly into the water, and to my great astonishment in a few minutes returned to the ship with the motionless animal in his mouth. Nor was this, I observed, a matter of such great difficulty as it appeared to my ignorance, and possibly may seem to that of my fresh-water reader. The kitten was now exposed to air and sun on deck, where its life, of which it retained no symptoms, was despaired of by all.

The captain's humanity, if may so call it, did not so totally destroy his philosophy as to make him yield himself up to affliction on this melancholy occasion. Having felt his loss like a man, he resolved to show that he could bear it like one; and having declared he had rather lost a cask of rum or brandy, betook himself to threshing at backgammon with the Portuguese friar, in which innocent amusement they had passed about two-thirds of their time.

But as I have, perhaps, a little too wantonly endeavoured to raise the passions of my readers in this narrative, I should think myself unpardonable if I concluded it without giving them the satisfaction of hearing that the kitten at last recovered, to the great joy of the good captain, but to the great disappointment of some of the sailors, who asserted that the drowning cat was the very surest way of raising a favourable wind; a supposition of which, though we have heard several plausible accounts, we will not presume to assign the true original reason.

From *The Journal of a Voyage to Lisbon* by Henry Fielding (1755).

Discussion or comprehension points could include:

- the sequence of events
- impressions formed of and about the writer
- the character of the captain
- how and why the kitten probably came to fall 'from a window into the water'
- long eighteenth century paragraphs and sentences and fussy punctuation. Quite a good exercise to 'edit' it for twenty-first century readers: leave the words but 'modernise' the punctuation
- words and expressions no longer used or changed in meaning.

If there is a subject – apart from love – which has inspired more literature and writing of all kinds than war then enlighten me because I don't what it is. Because war and its horrors (and perhaps a few positive angles, such as comradeship) are such timeless topics, people have been writing about them from every possible angle since Homer and before.

And some of the bloodiest war stories are in The Bible – a book of books I've long argued should be presented in English lessons as literature. As well as Byron's take on Sennacherib's defeat which appears in *English Year 9*, Chapter 4 (page 71), consider Jael's gruesome killing of the enemy Sisera (Judges, Chapter 4, verses 17–21). Or, beloved of many a painter – it's even on the Sistine Chapel ceiling courtesy of Michelangelo – Judith's decapitation of Holfernes (Judith, Chapter 13, verse 2). Even the more familiar David and Goliath (1 Samuel, Chapter 17) is a war story, among other things.

There are also – tragically – war stories, real, urgent, current ones in our newspapers every day. War, as George Bernard Shaw in his play 'Major Barbara' makes Undershaft assert repeatedly and joyfully (because he's an armaments millionaire) is a constant. It never goes away.

Need a good starting point for a discussion? Consider these two opposing views, separated by 2,000 years or so:

● 'We make a war that we may live in peace' (Aristotle, 384–322 BC).

● 'There never was a good war, or a bad peace' (Benjamin Franklin, 1783).

You and your pupils will not have to look far to find current or recent wars as examples.

The work in this chapter is, moreover, particularly useful as preparation for the start of next year's GCSE course when most pupils study some First World War poetry.

>> Task 4.1

1. Vasser has pricked her in the throat with a knife whose tip is poisoned. She described how it 'jabbed lightly' like a 'mild sting'. Vasser then tells her that 'the venom on my blade is slow acting'. The first effects are that her fingers and feet grow cold but paralysis is taking hold and she cannot move to warm them. She is beginning to lose consciousness.

2. Points to look for in a good answer include:

    ● physical strength 'strong-armed, battle hard'

    ● armed with both sword and knife

    ● described as 'like a young man' he isn't actually young. Anyway he is Beren's uncle

    ● skilled, tactical fighter in one-to-one combat, 'making brief passes in front of me with his knees, to keep me off centre'

    ● menacing – 'stone still as a hawk's head as she looks at her prey' and 'a venomous snake'

- sexual jealousy – Beren's mother preferred his weaker brother Thorkil

- harbours grudges – thinking about Beren's mother whom he claims ('I killed her, Beren') to have murdered

- cruel – wants Beren to die slowly and kicks her legs to make her fall.

3. Othinn is mentioned twice only. He will decide the outcome of the fight with Vasser and he is associated ('Othinn's fire') with the 'bloodsurge' of adrenalin (as we would now recognise it) which 'bathed' her and enabled her to find extra strength. He is, by inference, a god or deity. There is religious resignation in the words 'Othinn will decide the outcome'.

4. There are two main points to make about 'blood debt':

- The passage seems to imply that blood has been shed in the past and must now be shed again in payment. Vasser is quelling what he sees as a rebellion (line 55) by Beren and the fighters with her. By implication she is 'rebelling' because she feels she must avenge the killing of her own people in the past by killing the perpetrators.

- 'blood' can be taken to mean related to (in expressions such as 'blood relative' or 'He's not of our blood'). Vasser and Beren are related although they hate each other. Her feeling that she must make Vasser pay in blood is also to do with their relationship as uncle and niece.

>> Task 4.2

1. A full answer might include General Walker's:

- frankness: he declares the front 'no place for woman'

- punctiliousness: he takes the view that 'orders are orders' and assured the narrator of 'absolutely equal treatment'

- concern for his reputation and that of the US army: he will be criticised if anything happens to the narrator, so he asks her to 'be careful and don't get yourself captured or killed'

- skill as a tactician – determined not to retreat and makes good use of reinforcements, the Ist Cavalry and 25th Division: 'The operation was skilfully done' and 'a tribute to General Walker' that he was able 'to juggle his forces geographically so as to hold on to that great semicircle'.

2. To answer this question pupils need a good grasp of what happened at Dunkirk between 26 May and 4 June 1940 so you may need to discuss it at some length. Over 300,000 allied servicemen were rescued from the beaches and harbours around Dunkirk by military ships – and, famously, by over 700 small boats from England – as the German army moved across northern France towards the coast. They would have been trapped on the beaches and a sitting target for the Germans, had they not been rescued.

General Walker is determined to avoid a similar situation in Korea. That is why he insists that his men must 'stand or die' until reinforcements arrive. Were they to retreat, hundreds of Americans could be stranded at great risk on the coast near Pusan.

When Marguerite Higgins wrote this in 1951 the war in Europe and the events at Dunkirk were still quite recent memories.

3. There is a great deal pupils might find to comment on here. The points below are really only a selection of the points of comparison which might interest them:

   ● Higgins is allowed to do her job 'with no more hindrance than the men' once General Walker has told her his views. So thereafter we lose sight of her being a woman, she simply becomes a reporter and even uses the generic word 'newspaperman' to describe herself. Beren, too, is treated like a man. She fights and responds like one and what she lacks in physical strength she makes up for in agility – 'I was quick on my feet'. Both these women are, primarily, people doing a job on an equal footing with men. The fact that they are women is secondary.

   ● Beren is an active, hands-on fighter who, at one point, hears 'only the ding and dint of the iron as we traded blows edge to edge'. Thus she is quite different from Higgins who is describing the progress of the war as an outside observer (with time to record the beauty of the country (lines 69–71). She gives an overview and isn't close, at this stage in her narrative at least, to bloodshed.

   ● Pauline Chandler's graphic writing is very immediate and almost poetic 'To stab and stab and stab again' and 'stone still as a hawk's head'. Higgins is more concerned for a clear, measured explanation ('We attained a smaller, better-integrated defense arc') of what is going on. Her style has more precision although she uses apt metaphors such as 'barrelling' to describe troop movements.

   ● Fiction relies heavily on dialogue and there's a lot of it in the Pauline Chandler passage. The spoken words show us what the characters are doing, thinking, feeling and so on as well as making the narrative forge ahead like a play. Reportage, in contrast, depends on one person describing what he or she has seen, heard or experienced in a particular situation and sets out to be a truthful record for posterity. Higgins here uses the first person to stress that she is reporting from the centre of the action. Only once does she use reported speech (lines 10–18). This makes her style in Passage B seem slower and more thoughtful that the pulsing excitement which drives the fictional Passage A.

➤➤ Task 4.3

1. Look for these points:

   ● The Belgians were lined up in front of the (British) 5th Division.

   ● They were attacked.

   ● Those which tried to retaliate from the sidelines by breaking ranks ('their skirmishers') filtered out of sight through the 5th division.

   ● They ('were seen no more during the action') retreated and disappeared.

Strictly speaking, it goes beyond the scope of the question, but pupils might also like to comment on/write about what happened after the disappearance of the 10,000 Belgians: very rapid destruction of 2,000 French troops by the 92nd Division and the Scots Greys.

2. A selection (not an exhaustive list) of possible points:

- Both passages are full of factual detail, such as 'To fill the gap vacated by the 25th Division. The 1st Cavalry and the South Koreans were pulled back in a tightening operation' (Passage B, lines 56–57) and 'when they were immediately ordered to stand to their arms' (Passage C, line 21). This is because the writers were there to describe what they saw although Lieutenant Winchester is much closer to the action than Marguerite Higgins.

- 'The Enemy on reaching the hedge had shouldered arms' could not have been written by someone who wasn't present (other than in fiction). That, and similes, such as 'as green and smooth as the 15 acres in Phoenix Park' (Passage C, line 34) and images such as 'jewel-bright rice paddies' (Passage B, line 70), give great immediacy.

- Both passages use military vocabulary including words such as 'Division', 'regiment', 'defense arc' and 'shouldering'.

- Higgins, the professional journalist, is describing what she sees and is told, for readers back home. But she is clearly on the American side. There is nothing impartial in her writing. In the same way, Winchester, who is an amateur writer, is obviously on the British side referring to the French as the 'Enemy' and matter-of-factly recording that 2,000 of them were killed, wounded or captured in three minutes. Higgins says nothing about loss of life, perhaps because she hasn't seen it at first hand. Neither writer is disinterested or impartial.

- 'I would have gotten a terrible press' (Passage B, lines 11/12) and the American spelling of 'defense' are just two signs that Passage B is American English. Her style includes a number of incisive short sentences, too, such as the simple 'Their soldiers were not just battle-toughened' (line 34) and the compound 'So I left Pusan and hitchhiked my way west' (line 67) which make it seem modern. Passage C uses longer sentences – in the style of early nineteenth century British English – such as the complex, 68-word sentence beginning 'The Scots Greys came…' (line 28) which meanders its way through various subordinate clauses and phrases before reaching a full stop after 'Eagles captured' (line 33). For that reason, Winchester's writing needs more punctuation – especially commas and occasional semi-colons – than Higgins whose writing is quite sparely punctuated.

- Winchester's description is more precise than Higgins's because he is describing the events of a single hour. Her report covers several days and therefore is more of a summary than a blow-by-blow account.

>> Task 4.4

1. He offers a passport (line 19). Literally (and originally) it was an authorisation for the holder to pass through ports and across state boundaries. It would, in this case, have been a document signed by the king. Henry also promises that 'crowns for convoy' shall be 'put into his purse' which means that he will provide money to pay for the journey home for any man who wants to opt out of the fighting.

2. Henry argues that:

   - it is a great honour to fight (and perhaps die) for your country ('I would not lose so great an honour', line 14)

   - the smaller the force the more glory each man gets ('The fewer men, the greater share of honour', line 5)

   - survivors of the battle will look back at it with pride and boast for many years to come ('These wounds I had on Crispin's day', line 31)

   - will remember the romance of fighting alongside ('Harry the King', line 36) and the other nobles listed

   - even the humblest man ('be he ne'er so vile', line 45) is equal to the king ('we band of brothers', line 43) in this context

   - men who are not there ('in England now a-bed', line 47) will always regret ('shall think themselves accursed', line 48) not being there.

3. Points to look for in a full answer include:

   - compared with a predatory beast ('like the wolf on the fold')

   - dressed 'purple and gold' are the traditional colours of luxury, glamour and royalty

   - they stand out because they seem to shine; 'gleaming' and 'sheen'

   - they have a glittering, stellar quality like the stars over the sea of Galilee on a dark night

   - use of synecdoche – making the single word 'Assyrian' and the strong pronoun 'he' stand for the entire army.

4. The pupil is spoiled for choice in this deliciously rich poem. The task is open to almost any response. If it were me I'd go for these, but it's a very personal thing:

   - 'That host on the morrow lay withered and strown' (line 8). The repeated long 'o' sound in 'host', 'morrow' and the archaic 'strown' reinforce the shock and horror of what has happened and the 'withered and strown' image reduces the noble Assyrian army to fallen leaves. The word 'host' is interesting too because it is the usual collective noun for angels so it confers an angelic quality on these fallen men.

   - 'foam of his gasping' (line 15) is an intensely graphic image of a dying horse as it fights for its final bubbling breath. The possessive pronoun 'his' rather than 'its' invites sympathy for the horse, too. It (he) is presented as a sentient being not an object.

- 'The lances unlifted, the trumpets unblown' (line 20). The negativity here is very effective. Normally, the Assyrians would be energetically, regally, and perhaps triumphantly, lifting lances and blowing trumpets. As it is there is still, silent nothingness. The lances and trumpets lie untouched.

5. You could probably write a short book in response to this task (and perhaps someone has), so you probably need to keep pupil work on it within bounds.

Some suggested points of comparison to focus on:

- Passage D is a first person speech to fighting men but Passage E is a third person narrative account of an event. So the latter has a 'plot' and tells a story which the former doesn't.

- Passage D is written in iambic pentameter, that most natural, conversational and rhetorical form of verse. Passage B uses the very regular four-feet lines (tetrameters) the evenness of which evoke the sound of the marching of feet, the galloping of horses and the driving excitement, especially at the beginning.

- The tension on Passage D rests on anticipation of the battle yet to come. In passage E, we are there at the event with the poet and the lamenting widows who are 'loud in their wail'.

- Both passages are highly evocative and moving. 'We few, we happy few, we band of brothers' (Passage D, line 43) has the same kind of choked sadness as 'hath melted like snow in the glance of the Lord!' (Passage E, line 24).

6. This is a very open-ended question. All I can suggest are some obvious starting points. The last thing we want is to pre-empt pupils' responses by imposing views on them. And I wouldn't blame them if they said that both passages are, in their different ways, absolutely marvellous and that it is therefore an impossible choice – which would probably be my own reaction:

- Look at the imagery. Take Henry's imagined old men reminiscing 'in their flowing cups' and showing their war wounds decades from now. Consider Byron's comparison of the Assyrian army with the green leaves of summer being suddenly destroyed (by supernatural forces) as if by an autumn wind.

- Examine the rhythm of both passages. How well does Byron's jogging, even, four lines to a verse work? Is it the flexible iambic pentameter which makes the St Crispin speech the powerful piece of writing it is?

- The role of God in both passages. Henry mention's 'God's will' (line 6) and 'God's peace' (line 14). God will decide the ultimate outcome of the battle and perhaps he already has ('If we are mark'd to die', line 3) In Passage E it is God who has shown himself to be the enemy of the Assyrians and their idolatry in 'temple of Baal' which is, by inference, why he has sent his 'Angel of Death' to destroy them.

Writing about literature and Task 4.5

I think we sometimes forget the poetic qualities of fine prose such as we see in Passage A. In fact, is it always possible to draw a firm line between the two? Good prose has its own rhythm, as all language does, and is just as interesting to read closely as poetry. It is a fine foundation for anyone who later tackles A level English Language. Here's another example of analytical writing about prose to encourage your pupils. The sentence below comes from Passage B lines 52–54:

> **He sent them barrelling to the southwest front to bear the brunt of the enemy's attempt to break through to Pusan.**

The apparently effortless flow of this sentence is underpinned by the alliterative effect of the repeated 'b' in 'barrelling', 'bear', brunt' and 'break'. It is a plosive, too, which – added to the plosive 'P' of Pusan – adds an aggressive edge (reminiscent of gun fire) to what is being said. The image in the word 'barrelling' succinctly suggests the movement of troops in a big curve towards the southwest front. We can see exactly where the writer's allegiance lies through her use of the word 'enemy's' and we note that it was only an 'attempt' to break though. Even at this point the inference is that it was a failed attempt. The sentence has a very 'clean' uncluttered shape – a simple statement followed by an explanatory phrase – which adds to its directness.

Personal writing

Expressing your views in the form of an essay, and marshalling arguments within it, is quite a sophisticated skill – but one we need to develop for courses in various subjects later from GCSE through AS and A2 to, eventually, undergraduate work.

I have suggested a fairly pedestrian, banal approach (but it works for most) in *English Year 9* to get pupils started. But, of course, this rather formulaic method is not the only, or the best, way of writing a discursive essay.

As with so much of the writing we ask them to do, pupils will have a much clearer idea of what is being asked of them if they read a wide spectrum of examples. Steer them towards newspapers for this. Leader writers and columnists in quality newspapers such as **The Times**, **The Independent**, the **Guardian** and **The Daily Telegraph** write well-reasoned and argued 'essays' on a huge range of subjects. Use some of these as exemplars. In class I have found columns by **Libby Purves** (*The Times*), **Simon Heffer** (*The Daily Telegraph*) and **India Knight** (*The Sunday Times*) particularly useful. Look out for professional essays with plenty of 'attitude' but without bigotry.

> Be clear with the pupils, incidentally, about the difference between a leader and a column. A leader occupies a prominent, central place in the newspaper and carries no by-line. It purports to express the newspaper's corporate view and will often say something like 'This newspaper believes …'. An opinion-based column, on the other hand, consists of the personal views of the writer and is often more quirky in its expression than that of the – usually – more staid leaders.

Word bank

You can do these etymological treasure hunts with many words in English – all you need is a good dictionary and, perhaps, a Latin dictionary. Most pupils are fascinated by the origins of, and links between, words – especially if they haven't done any Latin. Then it's a wonderful discovery that language evolves and develops and that there is kaleidoscopic pattern in it.

That is why, by the way, I would never buy for school use a set of dictionaries without derivations as well as meanings. It is worth explaining this to parents, too, when they ask you to recommend a dictionary to buy for their son or daughter. I have Collins English Dictionary on my desk. It is a bit heavy to lift but indispensable and I use it countless times every day.

> Two more words from the Chapter 4 passages whose derivation and links are fun and good for extending vocabulary:
>
> - **regiment** (from the Latin *regere* to rule): links with regulate, regimen, regime, etc. and *la règle*, a ruler for drawing lines (among other meanings) in French
>
> - **proclaim** (from the Latin *pro*, before and *clamare* to shout): links with declaim, exclaim, claim, clamour, clamorous, etc.

›› Task 4.7

As usual these can only be exemplar sentences. Pupils will (and should) come up with their own:

1. After 23 years as Head it was very hard for Dr Peters to relinquish his position and retire.

2. If you can manage not to covet other people's things and achievements and be content with yourself as you are, you will probably be much happier.

3. The accoutrements of table tennis include bats, balls, non-slip shoes and nets.

4. An untuned or overloud public address system produces distorted sound.

5. When the two cars collided it was the Fiat which took the brunt of the impact.

6. The rapidity of the Titanic's sinking was what surprised many people most.

7. Some people regard the famous Kennedy family as accursed since they have suffered so much misfortune from the assassinations of John and Robert Kennedy to the death of John's son in an air accident.

8. Some Christian groups refer to their members not as a congregation but as a fellowship.

9. As the soldiers opened fire a volley of shots rang out.

10. The news from the war zone was quiet because there had been no action apart from a few skirmishes.

Nuts and bolts

'Shakespeare and Byron both wrote fine poetry which communicates and inspires.'
The adjective 'both' here refers to Shakespeare and Byron, the subject of the sentence. It could have been placed at the beginning of the sentence: 'Both Shakespeare and Byron…'. The sentence means that both men wrote fine poetry.

'Shakespeare and Byron wrote fine poetry which both communicates and inspires.'
Here 'both' is an adverb attached to the verbs 'communicates' and 'inspires'. The poetry of the two men has both qualities.

'Neither Shakespeare nor Byron wrote prose or expressed views about current events.'
The pair of words 'neither' and 'nor' are negatives linking Shakespeare and Byron. The sentence means that they have in common something that the two writers did *not* do.

'Shakespeare and Byron neither wrote prose nor expressed views about current events.'
The emphasis is slightly different here. The sentence assumes that Shakespeare and Byron are connected. Then it tells you what they, as a pair, did *not* do. Actually, it's a slightly misleading sentence because Shakespeare and Byron lived in different centuries and, obviously, didn't know each other. You could infer from this sentence that they worked together. It's all a matter of precision and fine tuning.

>> Task 4.9

Do not pre-empt this but if you need some starting points these sorts of sentences work well. Encourage them to be very free in the re-writing:

- My wife and I both dislike fish and chips.
- Neither Roxana nor Rani has read a poem by Keats or Shelley.
- When you've finished solving this problem you may either read or start your homework.

Nuts and bolts and Task 4.10

Of course, pupils will have been taught the use of the apostrophe many times before. Nonetheless there will be large numbers of pupils in Year 9 classes who often, or even routinely, get it wrong – not helped in the least by the widespread misuse of the apostrophe almost everywhere you look and the vexing habit of some computer spell checkers which will not allow *its,* always substituting *it's.*

Given the tendency (possibly born of uncomprehending desperation) some pupils have of scattering apostrophes all over the page more or less at random but especially when they see an s, I have started the explanation on pages 76–77 of *English Year 9* with an account of when *not* to use an apostrophe. And the exercise which follows includes a number of words ending with s which are neither possessive nor contractions.

Then I move on to a revision of the basic rules – making it as clear and simple as I know how. I hope it helps:

1. Lord Byron's poem 'The Destruction of Sennacherib' has its origins in *The Bible*.

2. Prince Charles and the Duchess of Cornwall opened the town's new shopping centre.

3. It's been a while since we met the twins' mother.

4. We've invited several actresses to our school's open day.

5. King Charles's reign ended abruptly in 1649.

6. Haven't you asked Thomas's sisters to the party?

More speaking and listening activities

I sometimes think that too much 'speaking and listening' work at all levels focuses on the former to the detriment of the latter. This is why I often suggest activities in which pupils have to listen to something someone tells them – an oral book review, for example – and then summarise it for someone else. You cannot do that effectively without listening very attentively.

The same idea underpins the **Henry V** suggestion here. Few teenagers are not entranced and moved by the Kenneth Branagh 1989 version. If they watch it with a brief to *listen* to the spoken word they will have a focus for their exposure to the film and it's a good aural exercise.

Wide range reading

And still they come. Recent war novels, or novels touching on it, which I have read and liked and/or been moved by since finishing *English Year 9* include these titles for teenagers:

- *Saving Rafael* by Leslie Wilson (Andersen, 2009). A gripping and deeply moving holocaust story set in 1940s Berlin. *Romeo and Juliet* with overtones of Anne Frank.

- *The Knife of Never Letting Go* by Patrick Ness (Walker, 2008). A compelling page turner about a boy living in another world, relentlessly pursued by an army, for reasons which eventually become clear although it's the first part of a trilogy and ends on a cliff-hanger. Very original.

- *Solitaire* by Bernard Ashley (Usborne, 2008). A contemporary shipwreck story with links to war in an imaginary African country, this book evolves into a nicely crafted tale of loyalty and deception, war and peace.

- *Fever Crumb* by Philip Reeve (Scholastic, 2009). A standalone 'prequel' to Reeve's *Mortal Engines* quartet, this is a fast paced fantasy in which London is days away from war in a world in which cities devour each other.

Additional passage

John Milton (1608–1674) generally needs no introduction, of course, but he probably will to Year 9 pupils. I find it's a good idea to present Milton in tiny amounts first – and the sonnets are ideal for this – mentioning the great 'Paradise Lost' in passing just to raise awareness that it's there waiting for them. Very keen/able pupils who might be ready to dip a tentative toe into 'Paradise Lost' could find Anton Lesser's recorded reading of it the best place to start. He read it for Radio 3, a book a day over Christmas 2008, and the whole work is now available on CD (Naxos Audiobooks).

Meanwhile, explain to them that Milton was a parliamentarian at the time of the English Civil War (cross-refer with Lovelace's poem on pages 10/11 of English Year 9) and a great admirer of Oliver Cromwell, a military leader who ruled England as Protector from 1653–1658 and one of the 100 or so signatories on Charles I's death warrant. Milton was Cromwell's Latin secretary – an interesting reflection on the way seventeenth century government was conducted that Cromwell needed one.

Antonia Fraser, incidentally, called her 1973 biography of Cromwell 'Our Chief of Men'.

Sonnet XVI

Cromwell, our chief of men, who through a cloud
   Not of war only but detractions rude,
Guided by faith and matchless fortitude
   To peace and truth thy glorious way hast ploughed,
And on the neck of crownèd Fortune[1] proud
   Hast reared God's trophies and his work pursued,
While Darwen stream,[2] with blood of Scots imbrued,
   And Dunbar field[3] resounds thy praises loud,
And Worcester's[4] laureate wreath; yet much remains
   To conquer still: peace hath her victories
No less renowned than war; new foes arise
   Threat'ning to bind our souls with secular chains.
Help us to save free conscience from the paw
   of hireling wolves[5] whose gospel is their maw.

John Milton (1652)

Notes:
[1] Charles I and his son
[2] Battle of Preston (17 August 1648)
[3] Battle of Dunbar (3 September 1650)
[4] Battle of Worcester (3 September 1651)
[5] People belonging to religious groups, especially some Puritan sects, opposed to parliamentarian actions.

Discussion or comprehension points could include:

- Milton's reasons for dubbing Cromwell 'Our chief of men'

- the rhyme scheme (ABBAABBA CDDCEE), different from Elsie Balme's sonnet in *English Year 9*, page 30, dividing the poem into an octave and a sestet. The effect this has on the poem's meaning

- the changed meaning of the word 'rude'

- the meaning of 'secular chains'

- the imagery in the last two lines.

Birds can be beautiful, mysterious, sinister, comic and zoologically fascinating – among many other things – so it's hardly surprising that so much has been written about them in all genres. And you won't have any difficulty at all extending bird-related reading if you and the pupils wish. The variety is astounding.

I didn't, for instance, include Laurie Lee's 'Sunken Evening' or Ted Hughes's 'Hawk Roosting' in *English Year 9*, much as I love them (and so do pupils), because I've used them in books before and it doesn't do to get samey. And 'the plaintive anthem' of Keats's nightingale and 'shrill delight' of Shelley's Skylark are out there waiting for you when your pupils are ready, although both poems are, of course, about a lot more than birds.

Do not forget newspapers as a source of bird literature either. Birds are quite often in the news, as in Passage A – because of rising or falling numbers, conservation programmes, changing habitats and so on – or you can find some quite lyrical essays in the nature or open air pages at weekends.

Look up via the paper's website, for example, Daniel Butler's piece 'Mathematical chaos at sunset', which was published on 21 February 2009 in *The Daily Telegraph*. It is about murmurations of starlings: those extraordinary, huge, cloudy patterns made by thousands of individuals moving in formation. The article is beautifully written and contains the words: 'A swirling, chattering flock of starlings swirls above the wetlands of Whixall Moss on the Welsh border, shimmering dark then light as it drifts like a plume of smoke from some monstrous pyre'.

For even more avian writing, dip into the book I warmly recommend on page 99 of *English Year 9*. Edited by Graeme Gibson, husband of the great Canadian novelist Margaret Atwood, *The Bedside Book of Birds* provides plenty to choose from. It is a delightfully wide ranging book which, like all good anthologies, is also quite idiosyncratic.

Another good thing about birds as a theme for English lessons is their universality. Every pupil will have seen and/or heard and thought about birds because wherever you live in the world birds are part of everyday life.

>> Task 5.1

1. 'Climate space' describes an area which has the right climate – temperatures, rainfall, wind and so on – to support a given species. Every animal, including birds, has physical needs which are controlled by the climate of its habitat. This is partly because a bird's food is dependent on climate. If it needs, say, berries, it has to live in a place where berries grow. If it becomes too hot for berries and the bushes die then berry-eating birds cannot thrive. If the climate changes in a place then some birds will be unable to live, feed and breed there, so they move to a different place which has the right climate for them.

2. Look for most of these points in a good answer:
    ● Three quarters of British bird species will decline in number.

- Eight species, including the snow bunting, pintail, Scottish crossbill and arctic skua, will disappear from Britain completely.
- Another eight species or so, including the red-throated diver and the dotterel, will lose 19 out of 20 specimens (95%), so levels will be very low.
- Many common birds, including redshanks, snipe and wading birds are likely to move northward and leave the warmer south of Britain.
- Overall, the distribution of most birds will shift about 340 miles to the north-east.
- Some birds, now limited to countries south of Britain which will also get warmer, may move northward into southern England in search of the climate they need. Possibilities include the serin, hoopoe, scops owl and black kite.

3. Professor Brian Huntley, Dr Yvonne Collingham and Dr Steve Willis of Durham University and Professor Rhys Green of Cambridge University and the RSPB want 'urgent action to combat climate change'. Director of the RSPB, Mark Avery, agrees. He says that we must 'act immediately to curb climate change'. Meanwhile, Professor Green advocates identifying 'species most at risk' so that their need of 'help and protection' can be met. Generally, however, the experts – according to this article, at least – are very quiet about exactly how climate change can be prevented.

4. Scientists have:
- worked out the winter and summer temperatures and moisture levels which each of 450 bird species needs or can tolerate
- put this information on maps
- taken 'climate models' prepared on sophisticated computers based on current global warming predictions
- used these computers to work out how each bird's habitat range will shift as the climate changes
- prepared a new set of maps – 'A Climatic Atlas of European Breeding Birds' to show the changes which lie ahead.

>> Task 5.2

1. A good answer might include these facts about the syrinx:
- lies at the base of a bird's windpipe at the point where it forks into each lung
- cuboid ('box-shaped')
- reinforced with cartilage bands
- contains two pairs of lips which can open and close the openings into the two tubes leading toward the lungs
- creates a musical note when lungs are contracted and air forced through the lips
- has muscles which mean it can vibrate each pair of lips separately to create a range of notes and sounds
- is exclusive to birds.

2.   The two characteristics mentioned here which differentiate birds from other animals are:

   ● No other animal has a syrinx.

   ● Birds can produce a longer, more varied and complex range of vocal sound than any other animal.

3.   A good answer might include:

   ● The cartilage-ringed windpipe links the bird's mouth cavity with the lungs via the syrinx.

   ● It can modify the sounds the bird makes. The larger and longer the windpipe the deeper the sound.

   ● In some larger birds the windpipe has loops – even passing across the breast bone in some cases – so that it acts like an orchestral brass instrument.

   ● Some birds can shorten their windpipes at will to create different sounds. As the windpipe shortens the pitch of the note rises.

   ● Others (penguins) have a partition running through the windpipe so that it can produce two notes at once – a chord.

4.   There is, obviously, a great deal which could be said about the presentation of scientific information to a non-technical audience and the different/similar ways in which these two writers handle it. What follows is really just a few starting-point ideas for comparison:

   ● Passage A is really about geography and the environment. Passage B presents zoological information. That means that, inevitably, Passage B hones in on anatomical detail whereas Passage A is looking at a much broader picture.

   ● Attenborough in Passage B demonstrates a real knack of explaining quite complicated physics by comparing the processes with those of familiar objects such as organ pipes, French horns, trumpets, boxes and lips. McCarthy's account of the computer mapping process in Passage A is not especially clear.

   ● Attenborough, because he is writing about song and sound uses a lot of musical vocabulary in Passage B ('chord', 'glissando', 'trombone-like') and the tone is quite informal. McCarthy uses more formal, often Latinate vocabulary such as '… factors other than climate can ultimately determine range, such as habitat availability and direct efforts at conservation'.

   ● McCarthy's sentences are generally longer and grammatically more complex in Passage A than Attenborough's in Passage B. This has the effect of making Passage A denser and less accessible. Passage B is actually quite entertaining. Passage A is much drier.

>> Task 5.3

1. Some of these points might be included in a good answer:

   - Eggbert's 'outsize feet' seem disproportionately large for the rest of his body.

   - They tend to foul each other when he walks so that he loses his balance.

   - Sometimes Eggbert appears to be gazing at his feet as if he is trying to get them under control ('So he kept close watch on them for any signs of insubordination').

   - When Eggbert tries to stalk butterflies he stops looking at his feet and falls into the daisies.

2. Screamer birds are 'supposed to be' herbivorous – presumably according to books and other expert sources. So the author is surprised when the bird's eyes develop 'a most un-vegetarian like gleam' as Eggbert tries to stalk any butterfly which comes nearer than six feet, apparently overtaken by 'blood-lust'.

3. Readers might deduce that Gerald Durrell:

   - has a strong sense of humour. The idea of this big clumsy bird being able to 'gambol about the lawn with the grace of a dried thistle-head' or trying to trick his own feet is witty. So is the notion that Eggbert's feet have minds of their own

   - is a careful observer of animal behaviour. He has watched Eggbert very closely to be able to describe his movements in such detail

   - readily finds a strong personality in Eggbert and empathises with the bird. He is seeing life from Eggbert's imagined point of view and identifying with the bird's apparent frustration when he writes that the feet 'would deliberately and maliciously twist themselves into a knot'

   - has studied the animals he is working with ('supposed to be entirely vegetarian')

   - is not working alone. He several times says 'we'

   - is a gifted writer with a real flair for words and images. Witness 'wiggled gently in the grass, spread out like the arms of a starfish' and 'his feet, left to their own devices would start to play up, treading on each other's toes, crossing over each other, and sometimes even trying to walk in the wrong directions'.

>> Task 5.4

1. The poet is admiring the single-minded, unthinking, totally focussed behaviour of thrushes which pull some 'writhing thing' from the ground with 'a start, a bounce, a stab' and comparing them with thoughtful, dreamy human beings. Before he kills for food or in war, a human will hesitate and moralise. In comparison with the thrush, this makes him seem lazy and inclined not to get on with things – 'indolent procrastinations' or he might seem slow and reluctant with his 'yawning stares'. This human need to create stories ('Heroisms on horseback'), works of art ('Carving at a tiny ivory ornament') or to be involved in religion ('bends to be blent in the prayer') makes

the experience of living much more complicated than it is for the 'single-mind-sized skull' of the thrush. In a sense Hughes is envying thrushes their 'bullet and automatic purpose' because they are, apparently, free of 'the distracting devils' which make human life anything but simple.

2.   Another wide open question. All I can offer you is what I would choose from this intensely sensuous poem, but your pupils should have ideas and views of their own:

- 'like a ruby rock' (line 2) is a very apt and accurate simile. It presents an image of the bird's glittering, unblinking, bright red eye. It also fits in with other imagery in the poem which presents the bird as an exotic creature made from precious metal 'gilded with thick-leaf paint' as if it were an ancient sculpture with an eye made from a ruby. The word 'rock' connotes a tactile hardness.

- 'The thrusting nut and bursting apple/accompany his jointed walk' is full of movement and the bird is in tune with the shifting of the ripening autumn fruit around it. The two gerundives – 'thrusting' and 'bursting' create an image of fullness breaking out almost aggressively and certainly unstoppably while the brightly coloured bird 'swaggers' around on the nearby banks on its stiffly articulated legs.

- 'this flushed October' personifies the season as 'ripe, and round-fleshed, and bellyful' – which makes the narrator feel warm and perhaps unwell ('Fevers me fast') but does not frighten him. There is something warm and reassuring in this cheerful image of the month which heralds winter.

3.   Obviously, this depends on personal interpretation and preference. A discussion before they write will almost certainly help. There is a great deal which could be said. Here are some starting points:

- In Passage D, Hughes is marvelling at the ruthlessness of birds which eat other creatures, and reflecting on the relatively inefficient introspection of human beings whose behaviour is governed by concepts of right and wrong. Lee, on the other hand, in Passage D, marvels at the regal beauty of the pheasant as part of an autumn scene and wonders why he, the narrator, isn't more apprehensive about the forthcoming winter. Perhaps it's worth noting, too, that many poets and writers have used the seasons of the year as a metaphor for a human life. Is Lee's narrator really surprised that he isn't frightened of his own forthcoming death: 'winter's skull'?

- Hughes's imagery is more succinct and sparer than Lee's. It has urgency about it. Chillingly, he compares the thrushes with 'coiled steel', for example, and then reveals why they're terrifying, each with a 'poised/dark deadly eye'. Lee's metaphors, on the other hand, seem gentler and more self-indulgent. The pheasant is on 'the cidrous banks of autumn' and when it 'blinks the lively dust of daylight' it is peacefully oblivious of the fact that, unlike a thrush, it is a game bird and likely to be shot ('the hunter's powder horn') and eaten.

- Although Hughes's poem in Passage D seems very freely expressed, it is actually quite tightly patterned in three eight line stanzas each ending with a short, powerful line. The form makes the poem seem reflective but controlled. Passage E looks more formal with its sixteen lines set out in four, four-line verses, but the rhythm is still free and, in its way, it is as reflective as Passage D.

- There is very little end rhyme in Passage D – which is what makes the verse seem free but the rhythm comes from alliteration ('sides too streamlined', 'distracting devils') and other effects such as the onomatopoeic 'a start, a bounce, a stab'. The first stanza is very dynamic, the second more thoughtful and the third quite inward-looking. The form allows the poet to move quite neatly from observation of nature to philosophical conjecture. Passage E uses the first three stanzas for colourful description before, like Passage D, moving off at a metaphysical tangent. Passage E has a more regular rhythm driven by a low key rhyme scheme in which alternate lines rhyme ('rock', 'cock', 'walk', 'stalk' and so on).

Writing about literature

It is, in my view, just as important to get Year 9 pupils writing critically, and in detail, about prose as it is about poetry because it helps to lay the foundations for the analytical work required in AS and A2 English Language work which many pupils will eventually need.

> Here is a second example of how pupils might comment on a paragraph of prose – the opening of Passage A:

> **If you're a bird-lover and you want to see nesting snow buntings in the mountains of Scotland, or pintail ducks breeding in the fens of East Anglia then go now; their time here is limited. Research shows that British and European birds face a potentially disastrous future thanks to climate change during the coming century.**

> Because this is a piece of newspaper journalism it has to 'hook' the reader at the beginning so he or she wants to read on. So the opening sentence is very direct and conversational. It uses the second person and an informal pronoun/verb construction – 'you're' – which creates a 'chatty' tone. It also flatters the reader by assuming educated, ornithological knowledge and familiarity with relatively unusual birds such as snow buntings and pintail ducks. The second half of the first sentence is a stark, monosyllabic warning 'then go now' with the drama of 'their time here is limited' heightened by the use of a semi-colon rather than a conjunction such as 'because' which would have been gentler and lessened the impact. The second sentence explains and expands on the warning by summarising what the rest of the article is about. It tells the reader what (birds), where (Britain and Europe), what (disastrous future), why (climate change), when (during the next 100 years). The most hopeful word in the whole paragraph is the adverb 'potentially' because it hints that none of this is certain.

Personal writing

There are some useful opportunities here to get pupils to write non-fiction with precision and with accuracy and attention to detail – a different skill, perhaps, from writing poetry (or maybe not – it too is very concise) or stories.

Many pupils are chary of using simple vocabulary because they begin to read widely and soon know lots of words. It therefore feels 'grown up' and 'clever' to write 'commence' when you mean 'start', 'consume' when you mean 'eat', 'cerulean' when you mean 'blue' or 'peregrinate' when you mean 'travel'.

In fact, as every English teacher knows, using long words, just for the sake of it (and often slightly misusing them) simply clutters your work and makes it read like verbose cotton wool.

So we have to work hard at teaching pupils that you need to know a lot of words in order to choose exactly the one you need, but that some of the best writers (Orwell, Hemingway, Camus) achieved magical effects with straightforward vocabulary and, generally, short sentences.

Orwell, too, argued against the use of unnecessary adverbs and adjectives.

It is worth drawing pupils' attention to this. Which is stronger: 'I am tired' or 'I am extremely tired'? 'He is an important man' or 'He is a very important man'? Which is more effective: 'He walked wearily' or 'He trudged'? 'I shouted extremely loudly' or 'I bellowed'? Get the right nouns and verbs and you don't need so many qualifiers.

It is also vital, I think, to get pupils into the habit of editing their own work with these points in mind. Train them to cut out everything which is unnecessary.

I tell pupils it reminds me of old-fashioned knicker elastic. When I was a child in austerity Britain, if the elastic went in your knickers you didn't throw them away. You got a new piece and threaded it loosely into the slot at the waistband with a safety pin. Then you pulled it tight until it was the right size for your waist before stitching it up. We have to do the same with our non-fiction writing – get it as tight as we can so that it fits perfectly. Most pupils enjoy the analogy.

Word bank

More delicious entymology. Other words from the passages in Chapter 5 which you could use as starting points include:

- **predict** (from Latin *prae* before and *dicere* to speak): links with contradict, dictation, dictaphone, diction, prepare, pre-book, prefer, preface, etc
- **vocalisation** (from Latin *vox, vocis*): links with voice, vocalist, vocal, vociferous
- **October** (from Latin *octo*): means eight, of course, because October was the eighth month in Early Roman times. Links with octagon, octopus, octave, octet, octogenarian.

>> Task 5.7

1. cataclysm: violent upheaval

2. magnification: enlargement or the process of making bigger

3. magnum: wine bottle double the size of a standard bottle

4. sequacious: logically following in regular sequence

5. cataplexy: sudden temporary paralysis

6. sequential: following in order

7.   magniloquent: lofty in speaking style

8.   obsequious: ingratiatingly attentive

›› Task 5.8

These are merely exemplar sentences. Pupils will have their own ideas:

1.   In *Twelfth Night*, Malvolio swaggers around the stage when he is duped into believing that Olivia is in love with him.

2.   The school fire alarm emits a loud buzz when it is tested.

3.   Because James has won three tennis matches in the tournament he is potentially regarded as an overall winner.

4.   The Statue of Liberty has iconic status as a symbol of the USA.

5.   My granny regards her arthritis as the bane of her life.

6.   When you draw your bow across a violin string the whole instrument resonates.

7.   I spent far too long teetering on the edge of the pool because I thought it would be cold.

8.   Paul had an erratic approach to his work last year but now he seems to be on a more even keel.

9.   The apple orchard overpowered us with its rotting, cidrous smell when we walked through it late last autumn.

10. Poor science A level results meant the demise of Rebecca's hope to study medicine.

11. A good bullet-proof vest can deflect most forms of ammunition.

12. Each time there is a new government, everyone hopes it will have some innovative ideas instead of relying on old, failed methods.

13. 'I am going to make you suffer for this,' said the bully, maliciously.

14. The audience was ready, attentive, anticipating a stunning evening with the visiting author.

15. My dad is pretty liberal and reasonable with us but he makes clear the parameters of what behaviour he will accept.

Nuts and bolts and Task 5.10

Direct and indirect speech have quite clear patterns and most pupils master the conventions fairly easily if you give them plenty of practice. They can do this simply by re-arranging pieces of text and altering the way dialogue is presented. It is quite empowering once a pupil realises just what scope there is.

Inevitably, there are many ways in which the play extract in Task 5.10 could be re-written as if in a novel. This is just one of them:

'Hey, leave them alone,' snapped Kelly, packing her bag, as Lucy tried to remove the headphones from her older sister's personal stereo on the table.

'They're mine,' replied Lucy. 'Look, they've got a blue mark on them.'

But Kelly crossly accused her of lying. 'You've broken yours. You know you have,' she said, putting the headphones in her bag as Lucy tried to snatch them, shouting that they were hers.

'They're mine,' insisted Kelly, ignoring Lucy's declaration of hatred and telling her forcefully to go away.

As Lucy stormed off muttering that Kelly already had two pairs while she had none, Kelly thought about the tiresomeness of little sisters, although deep down she knew that Lucy was right.

>> Task 5.11

1. There are fewer finches in British gardens than there used to be.

2. Less pollution would mean fewer losses of bird species.

3. Few scientists ignore global warming.

4. Less speed on the roads would result in fewer accidents.

5. Small birds need less space to take off than large ones.

6. There are now so few places to smoke that fewer people are buying cigarettes so there is much less friction between smokers and non-smokers.

>> Task 5.12

These sentences are just examples. Encourage the pupils to come up with their own. It will help to 'fix' the learning and discourage the sloppy use of 'literally':

- My English teacher owns literally thousands of books for which he needs 22 bookcases and various other storage cabinets.

- The wind on the headland was so strong that we were literally blown off our feet.

- I can play violin, cello and viola so I literally have several strings to my bow.

- Craig was so hungry that he literally ate everything in sight and when he'd finished every plate on the buffet was empty.

- We watched the dairy herd being moved and joked that we had literally waited until the cows came home.

- How literally should we take Fifi's offer to do anything she can to help us?

Wide range reading

Although there is a fair bit of bird-related fiction around and, of course, some splendid poetry, (did I mention William Cowper's eighteenth century **'The Jackdaw'**, Edward Lear's nineteenth century **'The Pelican Chorus'** and Douglas Livingstone's twentieth century **'Vulture'**?) it is in non-fiction that birds really fly.

Look, for example, at **The Encyclopaedia of Birds** edited by Christopher Perrins (new in paperback, Oxford University Press, 2009). It covers birds all over the world. The text is very readable and the photographs are terrific.

Two other useful reference (or dipping) books are **RSPB Handbook of British Birds** by Peter Holder and Tim Cleeves (2006) and **Birds Britannica** by Mark Cocker and Richard Mabey (Chatto & Windus, 2005).

Additional passage

Somehow, I couldn't find a way of including this unmissable little gem in English Year 9 so here it is now. Apart from anything else its brevity and (deceptive) simplicity make it a good poem for learning by heart for twenty-first century pupils who have been known to make heavy weather of learning poetry.

The Eagle

He clasps the crag with crooked hands;
Close to the sun in lonely lands,
Ring'd with the azure world, he stands.

The wrinkled sea beneath him crawls;
He watches from his mountain walls,
And like a thunderbolt he falls.

Alfred Lord Tennyson (1809–1892).

Discussion or comprehension points could include:

● effect of patterning created by the three line verses and two sets of three rhyming lines

● alliteration and what it adds to the poem

● anthropomorphism

● imagery such as 'wrinkled sea' and 'like a thunderbolt'

● comparison with Ted Hughes's widely anthologised 'Hawk Roosting'.

This is probably the most elastic theme in *English Year 9*. Since, as I tell pupils in the preamble to Chapter 6, work is anything which people have to do during an ordinary day whether it's salaried, domestic, self-employment or education-based, almost every text you pick up has a work element. So you can have tremendous fun with the versatility of it.

Novels are full of people working. The exploitative Sowerberrys and their spiteful apprentice, Noah Claypole, of Charles Dickens's *Oliver Twist* are all working in the undertaking business, for example. Mr Polly, of H G Wells's *The History of Mr Polly*, is a shop assistant and hates it. In Michael Morpurgo's 2008 story *The Mozart Question*, Paolo Levi is a working violinist. Joanna Trollope's 2000 novel *Marrying the Mistress* is about (among other things) the personal problems of a circuit judge and we see quite a lot of him at work. Or Minette Walters's 2006 novella *Chickenfeed*, based on the real 1924 'chicken farm murder' in East Sussex, has a chicken farmer as its central character. No, you really don't have to look far for work in fiction.

Poetry has plenty to offer, too. Do not miss, among many other possibilities if you want to broaden this topic out, W H Auden's 'Night Mail', Laurence Binyon's 'The Road-Menders', James Thomson's 'Sheep-Shearing', James Kirkup's 'All-in Wrestlers' and Leonard Clark's 'Bell Ringer'.

Then there's biography and autobiography. Any account of a life inevitably includes many passages about the subject's work. Nelson Mandela's *A Long Road to Freedom* (1994) is a treasure trove of extractable passages, for example. So is Barack Obama's *Dreams of My Father* (1995). Look, too, for biographies of, and autobiographies by, past and present sports people, actors, musicians, explorers, scientists, and so on.

In fact, you could quite easily theme a year's work on 'The World of Work'. Your biggest difficulty will probably be deciding where to stop.

>> Task 6.1

1. A full answer might include these points. Tess:

   - sits on the platform of the threshing machine

   - takes a bunch of tied-up corn stalks ('a sheaf of corn', line 12) from the woman next to her who passes it

   - unties the bunch as quickly as she can and hands it to a man who feeds it into a revolving drum which separates the grain from the stalks by shaking it at speed – a process known as threshing

   - does this repeatedly all day ('ceaselessness of the work', line 43) and, because of the noise, without speaking much ('prevented speech', lines 55–56) apart from during short meal breaks. 'For Tess there was no respite', line 48

   - has to work very quickly to ensure that that the process is continuous. If the drum revolves empty it is even noisier ('increased to a raving', line 56). She cannot even look up from what she is doing. 'Tess and the men who fed could never turn their heads', line 57).

2. Points to bring out include:

    ● 'Modern' threshing is done by placing the cut corn in a mechanically revolved drum.

    ● 'In the past – when the old men present were young – threshing involved beating by hand the corn stalks with flails on the wooden floor of the barn. The movement shook the grain free.

    ● 'Now with its 'inexorable wheels' and 'penetrating hum' threshing is very noisy and the vibrations shake everyone near to the drum 'to the very marrow' of their bones.

    ● 'The machine means that threshing can now be done very quickly but it's unpleasant (dehumanising, ignoble) hot, sweaty work for the operatives.

    ● 'Doing it by hand was slower but, according to the old men, it 'produced better results'.

3. Tess:

    ● is new to this work and already wishing 'that she had never come to Flintcomb Ash'

    ● has stamina, nimbleness and determination. Because she combines 'strength with quickness in untying, and both with staying power', Farmer Groby has selected her to be the un-tier who passes the corn to the men who feed it into the drum. Her presence keeps the process running efficiently and is therefore an 'economical' use of labour

    ● seems to be younger than the rest of the women, Marian, Izz and the others on the corn rick. They seem more resigned to the work, although they have an easier workload than Tess because they can stop for a few seconds to take a drink, speak, or brush away dust if they can. Marian may be sorry for the (younger, less experienced) Tess because she sometimes changes places with her for a short while although Farmer Groby objects

    ● is more attractive (refined) than the other women, or at least less coarsened by the work, because when they see the 'fancy man' in the corner of the field they are sure he has come for Tess.

>> Task 6.2

1. They are 'executioners' because they use axes to destroy tall, noble life by felling the oak tree.

    Hardy reinforces this by continuing to personify the tree, to invoke sympathy for it, and by using language associated with beheading and the death penalty:

    ● 'proud tree'

    ● 'death-mark'

    ● 'on its side'

    ● 'swing axes'

    ● 'broad deep gash'

    ● 'tall giant shivers'.

2. It would make sense to discuss this rather complex question before you ask pupils to write. Oral and/or written responses might include some of these observations:

- The sixteen line poem is divided into four four-line verses, each of which has a regular ABAB rhyming pattern within it. This helps to create a regular, predictable pulse which evokes the rhythm of the men's work as they 'stalk' and 'chop'.

- By linking end-rhyming words such as 'quivers' and 'shivers', which are close in meaning as well as in (onomatopoeic) sound, Hardy prolongs the image of the tree shaking before it falls especially as the word 'shivers' occurs twice more within lines 9 and 10.

- The link, in the last verse between the end-rhymed 'powers' and 'hours', adds to the pathos of the poem. We are listening for the rhyme with 'powers' and the 'less than two hours' in the final line is a sad anti-climax after the nobility of 'reached the end of its long staying powers'.

- In line 12, the half-rhyme of 'kneeling', 'sawing' and 'pulling' suggests the to-fro rhythm of the tree fellers' work.

3. As usual, give pupils a free rein and enjoy what they come up with. These would be my choices but it's very personal:

- 'Two executioners stalk': the emotive word 'executioners' at the very beginning of the poem makes Hardy's point of view instantly clear. He regards the legalised destruction – 'putting to death' as it were – of this innocent old tree as a form of murder. The verb 'stalk' which follows perfectly depicts the arrogant, unstoppable, determined advance of the executioners toward the condemned 'proud tree' which has been marked for felling ('death mark on its side').

- 'Lie white on moss and fallen leaves' as the tree is hacked to death 'chips fly about'. These fall on the dark 'moss and fallen leaves'. The word 'white' neatly and monosyllabically connotes the tree's innocence. It is a victim. The contrast of the fresh white with the weathered surroundings is also faintly obscene and repellent as if the tree's (usually) hidden interior is being violated.

- 'Then lastly, the living mast sways, further sways'. The alliterative 'l' here, combined with the hissing sibilance of all those 's' and 'st' sounds and the repetition of 'sways' conveys very effectively the slow-motion but inexorable toppling of the 'tall giant'. The language makes sure that we both hear it and see it as the tree's drama reaches its climax before, two lines later, it 'crashes downward'.

4. This is a very broad question with plenty of discussion potential. Encourage pupils to look closely at some or all of these points:

- Hardy's love of the countryside. Both passages have rural settings.

- Hardy's ultra-conservative, pessimistic, standpoint. He is very condemnatory of the threshing machine which Tess is working on. Despite its efficiency, the machine is presented as almost unbearable for her. Similarly the tree is, presumably, needed for timber, but Hardy sees only a 200-year-old 'tall giant' being arbitrarily 'executed'.

- Accuracy of description. The threshing machine ('the feeder could seize and spread it over the revolving drum, which whisked out every grain in one moment') and the tree felling process ('Till a broad gash in the bark is hewn out all the way round') are both very precisely observed.

- Mournful atmosphere in both passages stressed by words such as 'ceaselessness', 'inexorable' and 'severely' in Passage A and the menacing 'long limp two-handled saw' in Passage B. If this were music both would be in a minor key. Tess, from whose point of view much of Passage A is presented, is deeply unhappy and isolated. The narrator in Passage B regards the destruction of the tree as a death to mourn. Interestingly though, in both cases there are others present who are cheerfully getting on with what they have to do in contrast to Tess and the narrator of 'Throwing a Tree'.

>> Task 6.3

1. Traditional African farming:

    - is dependent on the weather

    - relies on hand tools and manpower rather than machines

    - has no method of irrigation

    - needs seed kept from the previous year's harvest (but sometimes farmers give each other seed as a form of currency)

    - uses natural methods and resources which happen to be there such as sisal rings to retain moisture

    - often means everyone in an area growing the same crop (yams, which are potato-like tubers, in this case).

2. Key points to look for in a good, short summary include:

    - freak weather conditions – first rains late and inadequate, followed by eight weeks of hot drought and then torrential rain without sunshine

    - if, like Okonkwo, you planted your yams during the first rains, the seedlings died in the drought

    - farmers who left planting until the second rains (and Okonkwo had some yams still to plant) saw most washed away in storms

    - the plants which survived didn't crop properly because there was no warmth to swell the tubers.

3. Differences in content between Passage A and Passage C include:

    - corn in the English countryside/yams in Nigeria

    - women working in farming/farming is clearly men's work

    - mechanised technology/farming by hand

- concerned with processing the harvest/worries about making crops grow and having a harvest at all

- threshing a sociable activity especially during meal breaks. Yam growing seems to be an individual way of farming

- evidence of farming methods changing/centuries old practices still the norm.

4. There is a lot to talk and write about here. These points are just that – starting points. My list is certainly not exhaustive:

- Achebe's sentences are much shorter than Hardy's. 'Some farmers had not planted their yams yet' (line 31). 'But the year had gone mad' (line 39). Compare these with Hardy's 51-word sentence (page 101, line 53) beginning 'For some probably…'. It has the effect of making Passage C seem much more direct. Does that make it more or less moving?

- One of the ways Achebe (like George Orwell and Ernest Hemingway whom I've mentioned before) achieves this spareness is by choosing strong nouns ('foresight', 'tendrils') and verbs ('scorched', 'sympathised') and avoiding gratuitous modifiers. Here Hardy is writing much more fluidly and formally than Achebe: 'Old men on the rising straw-rick talked of past days when they had been accustomed to thresh with flails on the oaken barn floor; when everything, even the winnowing was effected by hand-labour which, to their thinking, though slow, produced better results' (lines 34–40).

- Because he keeps his sentences short and rarely uses a dependent clause Achebe almost never needs punctuation within sentences. Hardy uses a large number of commas and semi-colons

- Achebe keeps his vocabulary simple. He uses conversational words such as 'sad' rather than 'tragic', 'lazy' rather than 'indolent' – whereas Hardy's more formal nineteenth century narrative includes words such as 'supplementary' and 'inexorable'.

- Achebe uses some colourful, apt images which seem appropriate to Okonkwo, such as comparing the scorched earth with hot coals (line 16) and his own strength to that of a lion. Passage A, in contrast, is almost free of figurative language.

- Both passages present despair largely through the viewpoint of one person although both are third person narratives which enable the author to refocus the view point if he wishes (as Hardy does at the end of Passage A).

An activity which might help:

- Get pupils to re-write a short section of one of the passages in the style of the other. For example, if Achebe had written it, the Hardy sentence I quote in my second bullet point above might have read:

   Old men on the rising rick talked of the past. They recalled threshing with flails on oaken barn floors. To them slow hand-labour was better.

>> Task 6.4

If pupils have already worked through Task 6.2 they will be 'on top' of Passage B so that much of the detailed preparation for this essay is done. Points about Passage D to be noted and compared could include:

- Lawrence is marvelling at – almost celebrating – the men who are making something 'faery and fine' rather than disapproving of their work as Hardy does of Job and Ike.

- Lawrence uses colour in a vivid painterly way with his 'blood-red' timber, 'blue of the morning,' 'red-gold spools' and 'cerulian mining'.

- Lawrence's men seem uplifted and ennobled (rather than demeaned like Hardy's 'executioners') by their work. They are also happy. He builds the sound of laughter into the last line with its alliterative 'l' sound and chuckling rhythm.

- Lawrence compares the railway workers with trolls as if they were in an otherworldly magical fairy tale 'at the cave of ringing cerulean mining' which is very different from the business-like way in which the tree fellers 'throw' Hardy's tree.

- Lawrence makes gentle, quite unobtrusive use of end rhyme in his eight line poem by rhyming the second and fourth line in both verses. The metre is fairly free, too, so we get a sense of the narrator's thoughtful stream-of-consciousness response unlike the regularity of Hardy's sad, angry 'sawing' rhythm.

- Both poems seem so immediate that they are almost certainly based on a specific, real life observed incident.

See, too, my short paragraph comparing two lines of Passage B with two lines of passage D in 'Writing about literature' on page 111 of *English Year 9*.

>> Task 6.5

1. A good full answer would probably take account of some or all of these points (among others). The narrator:

    - is curious; she evidently has not been into this room, the master's studio, before and is intrigued by it

    - makes and records detailed observations (like a seventeenth century Dutch painter): she describes the walls, the tiles ('not my father's'), furniture and painting equipment. These are her first impressions so they're very fresh

    - is unused to mirrors and is surprised by her own attractiveness ('I stared, surprised, then stepped away')

    - has clearly been schooled by her mother in how good maids work (line 63)

    - is conscientious and keen to do a good job ('I took up my broom' and 'but they had to be moved for the table really to be cleaned')

    - will ask for advice when she needs it: she is happy to consult Catherina (line 53)

- seems interested in the craft of painting: she describes her master's tools ('a knife with a diamond-shaped blade arranged on top to clean palettes') in detail and the items set out to be painted: 'a powderbrush, a pewter bowl, a letter, a black ceramic pot, blue cloth heaped to one side and hanging over the edge'.

2. Work done on Tasks 6.1 and 6.3, especially Task 6.3 question 4, will have furnished pupils with plenty of meat for this assignment. It is really just a case of helping them to identify the stylistic characteristics of Passage E which distinguish it from Passages A and C. For example Passage E:

- is a first person narrative

- uses, on the whole, simple short sentences (as Passage C does) because these purport to be the thoughts of an uneducated serving maid

- is very quiet, compared with Passages A and C because the narrator is working entirely alone; there is no dialogue

- is set indoors in a city – both the others feature farming and outdoor work

- seems more visual than Passages A and C, although the former describes the working of the thresher. The description in Passage C, 'bathed in light' from the window because the narrator has just opened the shutters, is – appropriately – like an artist's still life. It is very static. The only thing moving in the scene is the narrator who makes her character jump when she sees her own movement in the mirror

- has dramatic tension; at any moment the reader expects someone to come in and surprise her

- deals with just a few moments unlike Passage A which describes a whole working day and Passage C which summarises a whole season. That is why Passage E is more detailed – like a miniature pencil drawing compared with a big impressionist canvas with the paint slapped on.

>> Task 6.6

Pupils have already looked in detail at the style and content of Passages A, C and E. Points of comparison to bring out about Passage F include:

- use of language uncluttered with adjectives and adverbs

- precise information – 'He is paid 4s a-day ...' and 'As a matter of necessity every conductor must be able to read and write'

- third person description – Mayhew is observing the work not doing it himself

- no plot, drama or tension

- writing intended to educate and inform

- quotation in direct speech from a real conductor provides authenticity and corroborates the generalisations Mayhew has made

- glosses the street slang word 'cad' with which some of Mayhew's readers, especially Victorian ladies, would be unfamiliar

- clear explanation of what the job involves (the waybill and accounting for the money) rather as Hardy does fictionally with Tess in Passage A
- includes a record of the sorts of people who travel on omnibuses
- uses the first person so there's a sense of Mayhew, the journalist, carrying out 'on the ground' investigation.

Writing about literature

Comparing texts in writing in a detailed way is something many pupils find considerable difficulty with, although it is, in essence, just a knack which gets easier with practice. And they've already had several opportunities to compare and contrast – both orally and in writing – several times already in this chapter. This is just one more for luck.

The example I give on page 111 comparing a short section of the Hardy and Lawrence poems should already have helped to support Task 6.4 which is why I didn't set another separate task at this point in *English Year 9*. Here, however, is another example of how to compare two textual fragments. This time it's prose from Passages E and F:

With the windows open it was bright and airy, with whitewashed walls, and grey and white marble tiles on the floor, the darker tiles set in a pattern of square crosses. (Passage E, lines 19–24)

Among them are grocers, drapers, shopmen, barmen, printers, tailors, shoe-makers, clerks, joiners, saddlers, coach-builders, porters, town-travellers, carriers and fishmongers. (Passage F, lines 18–24)

Chevalier's complex sentence uses many adjectives – 'open', 'bright', 'airy', 'whitewashed', 'grey', 'white', 'marble', 'darker', 'square' – to make sure that her narrator's description is as clear and visual as possible. Mayhew is also concerned for accuracy but his emphasis is on facts rather than appearance. Hence the long list, separated by commas in a simple sentence, of the many different types who travel by omnibus. The fifteen items in his list are the subject (to the verb 'are') in his reversed sentence. It is clear and down to earth but neither chatty nor entertaining. Chevalier's sentence, on the other hand, gradually unfurls like a colourful fan all hanging on the subject 'it', a pronoun standing for the room.

Personal writing

As every English teacher knows, getting pupils to write worthwhile poetry is one of our toughest creative writing challenges. The title of Sandy Brownjohn's book ***Does it have to rhyme?*** (Hodder and Stoughton, 1980) says it all – and comes up, incidentally, with some useful ideas for teaching poetry.

I find – as explained in the 'Writing tip' on page 112 of *English Year 9* – that getting pupils to collect impressionistic mini-fragments works quite well as a starting point. Then let rhyme, alliteration and so on creep in naturally – or not – as the poem takes shape.

It is worth talking about rhyme and metre, too. Do we want the lines to be even or metrically patterned in some way or is the poem to be completely fluid?

As with all forms of writing the more pupils read writing of the genre they are trying to work in the more confident they will be. So if you want pupils to write good poetry, expose them to as much of it as you can.

>> Task 6.8

- drink/imbibe
- truthful/veracious
- happiness/felicity
- hunger/voracity

- bitter/acrimonious
- eat/consume
- enough/sufficient

>> Task 6.10

These are just examples. As always, encourage, pupils to make up their own – as quirky as they wish:

1. There was far too much loud coughing during the concert. (gerund)
   The coughing sound we heard in the night turned out to be a bullfrog. (gerundive)

2. Running is my favourite sport. (gerund)
   What is the running time of the film we're going to see? (gerundive)

3. During the counting of the votes the candidates paced up and down nervously. (gerund)
   The rhyme 'Sing a Song of Sixpence' finds the King in his counting house. (gerundive)

4. Dreaming is supposed to be good for you. (gerund)
   The poet Matthew Arnold described the 'dreaming towers' of Oxford. (gerundive)

5. The swinging to and fro of the broken shed door in the wind kept us all awake. (gerund)
   A pendulum is a weighted swinging device in a clock. (gerundive)

6. Circling is a feature of nearly all traditional dancing worldwide. (gerund)
   We watched the circling plane above the flying club. (gerundive)

7. Many girls used to learn shorthand and typing in schools and colleges. (gerund)
   How are your typing skills? (gerundive)

8. My grandmother, who is very economical, is always happy to do the mending. (gerund)
   Do you have any mending jobs for me today? (gerundive)

>> Task 6.11

These, obviously, are just examples, too:

1.   The **clapping** at the end of the play was quite overwhelming. (gerund)

2.   'I think I've had enough of your **questioning** for the moment', said our exhausted mother. (gerund)

3.   **Tumbling** share prices and interest rates are signs that a country has economic problems. (gerundive)

4.   'We have **rising** pressure so there's good weather on the way', observed the weather forecaster. (gerundive)

5.   The **dining** room is not used much except when we have guests. (gerundive)

6.   **Sleeping** is my cat's favourite activity. (gerund)

7.   Every child should have **swimming** lessons. (gerundive)

8.   The school library is a good place for quiet **reading**. (gerund)

Get it right and Task 6.12

A couple of hairy old chestnuts here that you will have taught, and pupils will have learned (or failed to) many times before. The only consolation, I find, is that each time you go back to it – if you vary your explanation – you pick up one or two more pupils who suddenly say, 'Oh! I see!' in delight as the light dawns. So it's worth all the tiresome repetition.

On pages 114 and 115 I have tried to explain effect/affect and laying/lying as clearly as I can. I hope it helps you and reaches some corners of your classroom which other explanations have failed to reach.

You could also point out that the transitive verb 'to lay' is linked with the word 'layer' so it means laying things down, perhaps in layers.

A few examples to help with Task 6.12:

effect/affect:

● We are seeing the effects of global warming.

● Carbon emissions affect global warming.

● Notice how D H Lawrence's use of colour contributes to the overall effect of 'Morning Work'.

● How much do you think metaphors affect meaning in poetry?

● Will the rail strike affect your grandfather's visit?

● We are studying the effects of the Second World War on the British economy.

lay/lie/laid/lain/lied/laying/lying:

- Is the table laid for dinner?

- Fred Atkins is a bricklayer.

- I had lain in bed for two hours before I fell asleep.

- Is that politician lying to us again?

- She lay very still and listened to every sound.

- The snow lay on the ground for several days last week.

- Our hens are laying well at the moment.

- Lie down and go to sleep.

- Lay the sheets of paper on top of each other, please.

- Five six, pick up sticks. Seven eight lay them straight.

More speaking and listening activities

Never underestimate the power of good reading aloud and encourage pupils to practise and rehearse it. If you can, get a really proficient reader aloud to demonstrate and/or run a workshop with the pupils. Most actors are very skilled at this.

Notice, too (politely, of course, if you have invited one to your school), how poor some writers are at reading their own work to audiences. Or listen to Simon Armitage or Carol Ann Duffy (poet Laureate until 2019) on the radio. Neither is a good poetry reader. After the visit/listening session it might be worth discussing with pupils why this might be. Is it a disdain for being 'theatrical'? Do they think the work speaks for itself without interpretation? Are they embarrassed to be reading their own words?

Of course, happily, there are many exceptions to this and some authors and poets are first-rate, very entertaining performers of their own work. Think of Pam Ayres. Incidentally, Wendy Cope, the poet (who is an excellent deliverer of her own verse), argues that no poet should need to *read* aloud his or her own work anyway. It should be firmly in the memory of its creator. Is she right? It could be another discussion topic for the pupils.

Wide range reading

My difficulty in compiling the list on pages 117 and 118 of *English Year 9* was knowing where to stop because, as I observed in the introduction to this section, The World of Work is such a vast subject. It is almost a case of think of a job – manual, office-based, craft-based, 'professional', or any other form of occupation – and you won't have to look far to find it in a novel or autobiography.

At the time of writing, for example, I am deep in A S Byatt's wonderful new novel **The Children's Book** (Chatto and Windus, 2009). Already I have noticed several, immaculately researched passages about working in the Natural History Museum when it first opened, being a children's novelist in late nineteenth century England and working in the Staffordshire potteries during the same period.

And I've just reviewed the re-publication of actor Sir Antony Sher's memoir **Beside Myself** (Nick Hern Books, 2009). Sher has published four novels and several theatre books so he is a real writer and certainly not just an actor who dabbles. His beautifully written memoir is, among other things, very strong on how actors work. A mild health warning, however: it contains elements which some teachers will consider unsuitable for Year 9. Read it and see what you think before you recommend it.

Since work of some sort features in almost every book it would be a good idea to get pupils to build up their own collaborative list of recommendations – perhaps providing a one or two sentence summary and an indication of what sort of work the book relates to.

Additional passage

Yet another form of work. Teacher, author, poet, teacher-trainer and now a hall-filling entertainer – and the funniest after-dinner speaker I have ever heard – Gervase Phinn worked for many years as a school inspector in rural Yorkshire. Here he describes visiting a tiny school in a remote spot in the Dales – education's answer to James Herriot? This passage comes from the first in a series about Phinn's work.

There were sixteen bright-eyed children ranging between seven and eleven who listened attentively to Mrs Brown as she explained the first task of the day which was concerned with some number work. I sat in the small reading corner and, in the course of the first hour, heard one child after another read to me, first from their own book and then from some I had brought. I asked the younger pupils to read to me from *The Tale of Peter Rabbit*, the children's classic by Beatrix Potter. The selection of this book, I found, was singularly unfortunate and I came to appreciate just how shrewd, bluntly honest and witty the Dales children can be.

John, a serious little boy of about seven or eight with a tangled mop of straw-coloured hair, was clearly not enamoured with the plot. He had arrived at that part of the story when poor Peter Rabbit, to escape the terrifying Mr McGregor who was searching for him in the vegetable garden, had become entangled in the gooseberry net. The frightened little rabbit had given himself up for lost and was shedding big tears. It was the climax to the story and when I read this part to my little nephew Jamie and my niece Kirsten, their eyes had widened like saucers and their mouths had fallen open in expectation of the capture of the poor little rabbit by the cruel gardener. But John, having faltered in his reading, stared impassively at me with tight little lips and wide staring eyes.

'What a terrible thing it would be,' I said, hoping to encourage him on again, 'if poor Peter Rabbit should be caught.'

'Rabbits! Rabbits!' cried the angry-faced little lad, scratching the tangled mop of hair in irritation. 'They're a blasted nuisance, that's what my dad says! Have you seen what rabbits do to a rape crop?' I answered that I had not. 'Rabbits with cotton-wool tails and pipe cleaner whiskers,' he sneered, 'and fur as soft as velvet. Huh! We shoot 'em! They can eat their way through a rape crop in a week, can rabbits. Clear nine acres in a month! Millions of pounds' worth of damage when it's a mild winter. No amount of fencing will stop 'em.'

'We gas ours,' added the little girl of about ten with round cheeks and closely-cropped red hair whom I had met earlier, and who was sitting nearby. 'That stops 'em I can tell you.'

'Nay, Marianne,' retorted the boy curling a small lip, 'gassin' doesn't work.' Then, looking me straight in the eye he added, 'Never mind poor Peter Rabbit. It's Mr MacGregor I feel sorry for – trying to grow his vegetables with a lot of 'ungry rabbits all ovver t'place'!

'Perhaps we should choose another book,' I suggested feebly.

At morning break Mrs Brown told me that John lived on a farm way out across the moors. It was a hard but happy life he led. He was expected, like most children from farming families, to help around the farm – feed the chickens, stack wood, muck out and undertake a whole host of other necessary jobs, and all that before starting his homework. He was a shrewd, good-natured, blunt-speaking little boy with a host of stories to tell about farm life. When he was little, Mrs Brown told me, he had been awakened by his father one night and taken into the byre to see the birth of a black Angus calf. The vet had suggested that it was about time the boy saw this miracle of nature. John had stood on a bale of hay in the cattle shed, staring in the half light as the great cow strained to deliver her calf. The small, wet, furry bundle soon arrived and the vet, wet with perspiration and with a triumphant look on his face, had gently wiped the calf's mouth and then held up the new-born creature for the little boy to see. John had stared wide-eyed.

'What do you think of that?' the vet had asked him. 'Isn't that a wonderful sight?'.

John had thought for a moment before replying. 'How did it swallow the dog in the first place?' he had asked.

From *The Other Side of the Dale* by Gervase Phinn (Michael Joseph, 1998).

Discussion or comprehension points could include:

- why the book choice was 'unfortunate'
- Phinn's affectionate tone and how he achieves it
- the humble way he shows himself up as ignorant in comparison with a child of eight
- his use of understatement
- his humour and delivery of the 'punch line' at the end
- his use of dialogue
- the extent to which this must be a partly fictionalised account based on real events.

Perhaps – given the large country's complex history and geography – it isn't all that surprising that the India-related literature is so rich. Kipling may be a very obvious choice to illustrate the point but his writing is an excellent choice to start this topic. Try reading Riki Tiki Tavi (from *The Jungle Book*) aloud, for example. It takes 40 minutes but it's worth it. I have never known a Year 9 class less than enraptured with it and I once had an impassioned request to read it in a Year 10 lesson because their friends in my Year 9 class had enthused about it so much. Apart from the gripping story with its life and death tussle, the Indian atmosphere in the garden with its plants and wildlife is beautifully done.

In Chapter 7 of *English Year 9* most of the passages are fairly upbeat which is why you really need, for balance, the very dark additional passages given at the end of this chapter. It would also make sense to broaden the topic with some focus on India's ongoing, grinding poverty which I refer to only in passing in the introduction.

A great deal has been written, for instance, about children who live in India's railway stations – in newspapers, for example – and about the stark contrasts in India between rich (largely thanks to the electronic revolution) and the poor. Rohinton Mistry's *A Fine Balance*, from which Passage B comes is a good source for a (fictional but accurate) slant on street life. You could get some valuable discussion – and preparation for GCSE oral work – from this. Or, since the text of *English Year 9* was finished we have had Danny Boyle's award-winning film *Slumdog Millionaire* (2008) – another potentially useful starting point for oral work.

>> Task 7.1

1. This is a good opportunity for some really catchy thinking and I suspect pupils will come up with something a lot better than I could. No catch-line writer, I cannot get beyond rather dull headings such as 'Tibet alive and well in North India' or 'Races mingle in the Himalayas'.

2. Contrasts include:
   - prosperous tourists ('well-shod, middle aged') and Buddhist monks
   - beer-drinking, 'sunburnt and travel weary', European gap-year students and atmosphere of holiness
   - colours of market merchandise and monks' robes ('clash gorgeously')
   - traditionally dressed monks with modern mobile phones.

3. The present tense:
   - conveys immediacy
   - gives the writing the quality of a diary
   - helps to make the article convincingly impressionistic; we really believe she is there
   - is quite usual in travel journalism.

The use of the second person/vocative/you:

- draws the reader in directly

- is a device to make the reader feel as if he/she is there with the writer

- creates an informal intimacy between writer and reader and makes the reader more likely to believe the writer

- implies that the reader really might go to McLeod Ganj and share Clover Stroud's experiences

- is common in travel journalism.

4. (a) 'an epicentre' is a metaphor borrowed from seismology (study of earthquakes) and implies that McLeod Ganj is the starting point for waves of influence which ripple a long way and very strongly. The writer is comparing the worldwide influence of Tibetan politics and culture with an earthquake. 'Focus' or 'centre' would have conveyed the same point about the key role of McLeod Ganj and the Dalai Lama's residence there, but the statement would have been weaker and less effective without the earthquake image. On the other hand, earthquakes are violent and destructive and Buddhism is gentle and benign, so perhaps it is not a wholly appropriate metaphor.

   (b) 'stacked up like Lego' nicely conveys the haphazard, unplanned and, perhaps, untidy growth of the monastic complex to a mostly British audience who will all be familiar with Lego's multicoloured angularity and capacity for hooking onto pieces of itself. The faintly childish simile also suggests the ad hoc nature of the building which has grown gradually to meet the needs of the monks whose numbers have risen over the years.

   (c) 'crows the size of dogs' is a rather repellent piece of hyperbole to stress that the crows are very big and well fed. It emphasises just how unpleasant the birds are as they peck opportunely at the grain mixed with butter. Dogs – or at least scavenging street dogs in India – are unattractive, potentially aggressive and possibly rabid so the writer clearly does not like the look of these big birds and wants to communicate that.

>> Task 7.2

1. The market place:

   - is full of fortune tellers including palmists, astrologers and less orthodox practitioners including people with card-picking doves, chart-reading parrots, communicating cows and diagram-divining snakes

   - is not a respectable place to go ('Always worried that an acquaintance would spot him')

   - is volatile, and the author is afraid that he might be caught in a riot

   - has some star attractions, such as the cow which appears to be answering questions

   - attracts gullible people, if they are taken in by such obvious con tricks.

2.   A good answer might notice the:

   - leading in of the cow to make a dramatic entrance

   - brightly coloured cloth wraps on the beast ('caparisoned in colourful brocaded fabrics')

   - contrasting effect of the light, tinkling bells with the 'bleating', 'groaning' and 'wailing' sound of the rubbed drum

   - repeated theatrical circling of the animal while its owner shouts a list of the cow's previous 'prophecies and forecasts'

   - calculated behaviour of the owner with his 'manic gestures' and 'frenzy' which contrasts with the 'cow's calm demeanour'.

3.   The author is not taken in by the fortune telling. He thinks it is just theatrical trickery and very easily seen through. So he pokes fun at it and at the people who are fooled or pretend to be. His tone is fairly jocular and a little lofty – as if he regards himself as above this sort of thing. Evidence for this includes:

   - the comparison of fortune tellers with 'stronger drugs' (line 13). He can see that going to the fortune tellers resembles the sort of shallow, but addictive escapism which comes from drug taking

   - comparing the excursions with auguries – a deliberate, pompous reference to the augurs, Roman religious officials whose job was to study the auspices and declare whether or not the gods favoured a proposed course of action. The gentle joke here is that they are avian auguries – just birds but believed with laughable seriousness

   - the description of the animal's past achievements as the 'cow's curriculum vitae' (line 39) which jokingly pretends – using irony – to take the recitation seriously. He continues this joke with 'brief biography' (line 41)

   - the witty use of alliteration signals his attitude: 'communicating cows, diagram-divining snakes', 'boorish bellowing'

   - sympathy for, and empathy with, the mistreated cow and 'the annoying drum that she had put up with for years'

   - sense that the author is quite pleased when the cow, at last, retaliates and 'gored her keeper with her vermilioned horns' later 'trampling him thoroughly'. He is on the cow's side.

4.   Both passages:

   - describe a market place

   - use colour to bring the description visually to life

   - mention small vivid things such as 'the path cluttered with flags' (Passage A, line 46) and 'soft, brown unprotected ear' (Passage B, line 53)

   - depict sounds.

But unlike Passage B, Passage A:

- uses the author's personal voice

- is factual although very impressionistic

- mentions smell – 'hot stink' (line 45)

- relies quite heavily on adjectives, adverbs and imagery.

And Passage B, unlike Passage A:

- uses humour

- is a fictional account written in the third person

- is part of a longer story and not a finished article

- uses fewer adjectives, adverbs and figurative language

- is more formal and 'literary' with less everyday vocabulary – 'curriculum vitae', 'demeanour', 'auguries', 'eldritch'.

>> Task 7.3

1. Points to bring out include:

   - supervisor of Protestant mission schools in Mayapore

   - effectively a missionary (to the Indians) responsible for education

   - by inference, educated and commited to Christianity

   - had, until now, trusted the peace-advocating Gandhi to work with the British against the grain of most other people's opinions

   - long regarded by the local British as a bit disloyal because she is friendly with Indians

   - wants to trust human nature but feels let down by Gandhi's (hyprocritical?) approval of Japanese action in Burma

   - removes Gandhi's picture from her study wall to make the point that she no longer supports him

   - is upset when the Indian ladies no longer want to visit her

   - seems to be a figure of fun ('diverse and cranky', line 33) to the British ex-patriot community

   - now invites British soldiers to tea to show solidarity – or perhaps because she is lonely and upset at being shunned by the ladies?

2. These questions are open to a range of valid responses. The key thing, of course, is to encourage pupils to be aware of the effect of style decisions such as the use of reported indirect speech in Passage C. Things to note about the style might include:

   - It gives the author the chance to change viewpoints. The second paragraph looks at Miss Crane's position from a distance via the collective impressions and thoughts of the people at the club. After that, like a camera moving in, we are with Miss Crane finding out what had really happened and her feelings about it.

- If you use direct speech there has to be more than one person present to create a dialogue and the author has to create 'scenes'. Instead, Scott has given us a summary, or overview, so that we know the general trend of events without having been 'present' at any specific occasion. That means he can cover the events of several weeks or months in a few paragraphs and move his narrative on.

- It allows the author easily to share Miss Crane's thoughts with the reader: 'Miss Crane suspected…' (line 35), 'She was sorry…' (line 41), 'she could only assume he was out of his senses…' (line 48).

3. The market (bazaar) in Passage C is:

- only in the narrative as a communal meeting place so that Miss Crane can be 'seen' encountering the ladies on neutral ground

- not presented atmospherically as the market places are in Passages A and B

- marginal to the passage rather than at its centre.

Note: the whole style of Passage C is different from Passages A and B, anyway. It has very little local colour and there is nothing of the smells and sounds of India. The focus of Passage C is political – showing how major global or national events affect the everyday lives of ordinary people as India inches toward independence.

›› Task 7.4

1. Aware that there is a time delay between India and Britain, Kipling contrasts:

- the 'saffron yellow' dawn of an Indian morning, its parrot calls, white dust and stenches with traditional Christmas eve 'making merry 'neath the white and scarlet berry'

- a morning funeral procession headed by a cattle-drawn bier toward the 'curling wreaths of smoke' pyre, with the singing of 'Good Christian men rejoice' from a hymnbook

- hot sunshine at 'high noon behind the tamarisks' with the cool pale daybreak ('breaking wan') in Britain on Christmas Day. Thinking ahead to Christmas dinner, he imagines British friends and relations who will 'drink our healths at dinner'.

2. The mood is, evidently, very dark. The narrator is deeply unhappy and feeling very negative about India where he doesn't want to be.

Every verse has emotive words which reinforce this message such as:

- dim, stenches, clammy, exiles

- crawl, past, appeal

- wan, toil, ceaseless, aching, alien

- sinking, shackled, tether, tattered, grim

- scream, bray, fruitless, hopeless, sadness.

Some words such as 'scream and bray' (compare with the drum sounds in Passage B) also have an onomatopoeic impact so that they sound like a howl of misery.

Words such as 'forget' and the repetition of 'Home' with its upper case initial letter add to the sense of acute homesickness, too.

3a. He is personifying India as a stepmother in a play on the traditional idea of your native country being your 'fatherland'. A Briton in India is a long way from his fatherland but is in a country which his father (Britain) has 'married' or colonised. Thus India becomes a stepmother, but as with many (traditional) stepmothers, the narrator is finding her enforced company less than congenial. She is 'grim' and she's been around a long time so she is scruffy and unappealing in her 'ancient and tattered raiment'. 'Hard her service and poor her payment', she is also very demanding. She expects a great deal from her 'kind' and the rewards are few.

b. We do not choose our stepmothers. They are chosen by fathers and we, the children, have to live with the consequences. The narrator seems to be very bitter about having to be in India, against his will serving this 'grim stepmother'.

4. Starting points for discussion/writing include:

- The rhythmic evenness of the poem with its five verses of eight lines each. Each verse has an ABABCDCD rhyme pattern.

- The relentless symmetry which helps create a soulful atmosphere as you wait for the negative, rhyming, last line in each verse.

- The internal rhyme in the fifth and seventh lines of each verse ('highway', 'byway', 'labours', 'neighbours', 'merry', 'berry', 'lent her', 'enter', and so on) which makes a sort of hiccough in the rhythm which hastens the verse towards its climax – the downbeat last line.

- It is a tribute to Kipling's technical skill as a poet that he could write to such a tight structure without the poem sounding forced. Do you/the pupils agree?

Writing about literature

Lead pupils toward A level literary criticism by the nose. Here is another example – '*pour encourager les autres*', as Voltaire said – of how one might comment in detail on a sentence of prose. This one is from Passage B, lines 40–42:

His voice was deafeningly raucous, his eyes bloodshot, his gestures manic, and all this frenzy was calculated as a masterly counterpoint to the cow's calm demeanour.

This compound sentence is constructed in two halves. First we get a list separated by commas giving us three pieces of information about the man's voice, eyes and gestures. The second half pivots on the conjunction 'and', when we are told about the cow whose 'calm' is dramatically different from the owner's frenzy. It implies that the man is a very convincing actor whose 'raucous' and 'manic' performance is 'calculated' and 'masterly'.

At the same time the omniscient author makes his own scepticism clear. He can see through this performance although he admires it. He distances himself with educated words, such as 'counterpoint', a term borrowed from Western music meaning two different melodies running at the same time. He means that the cow's quiet is like a different strand of the man's 'music'. They are working harmoniously together. The alliterative linking of 'calculated', 'counterpoint', 'cow's' and 'calm' adds to the sense that the author isn't taking this as seriously as some of the fictional onlookers in the market place do.

>> Task 7.7

1. Tempo: the Italian word for time. Used in music to mean the speed at which something is performed. Traditionally, all the instructions on music (crescendo, fortissimo, etc.) are in Italian. 'Tempo' is sometimes borrowed from music and used metaphorically.

2. Restaurant: French word for an eating place, cf café. Many English words relating to food come from French (menu, courgette, à la carte, etc.) because French, right back to the Norman Conquest, was seen as more elegant. Thus blanqette d'angeau instead of mutton stew, sous chef instead of under cook, petit pois instead of small peas.

3. Tofu: Japanese word for solid bean curd made from soya-bean milk. Has cheese-like consistency and is quite popular all over the world, especially with vegetarians. Because the Japanese invented it (and eat a great deal of it) it has a Japanese name. The spelling can vary.

4. Blitz: a corruption of the German word for lightning. Means a lightning attack and was used to describe the air attacks on London in the Second World War. Now both a noun and a verb in a widening range of contexts – some of them metaphorical ('I'm going to have a blitz of my bedroom this weekend because it's such a mess').

5. Safari: Swahili word for a journey. In English it now means a trip to a rural area, usually in Africa, to watch wildlife. Some stately homes in Britain (e.g. Woburn and Longleat) style themselves as 'safari parks' because they have exotic, uncaged wildlife.

6. Paparazzi: from the Italian word for freelance photographers specialising in candid camera shots of famous people and often involving invasion of privacy. Singular is paparazzo.

7. Pyjamas: from the Persian words for foot/leg and clothing. Originally referred to loose comfortable trousers worn by men in very hot countries in the Middle East. Word borrowed and eventually applied to nightwear with loose trousers.

8. Potato: from the Spanish patata. Sir Walter Raleigh found potatoes in South America in the sixteenth century and brought some home. The Spanish name came to Britain with the vegetable.

9. Anorak: from an Inuit word for a thick jacket with hood to keep out arctic winds. People who wear the British padded version have come to be jokily (perhaps unfairly) regarded as dull and old-fashioned with boring hobbies. So 'an anorak' – a nice example of metonymy and of how word meanings develop – is also a boring person.

10. Poncho: from American-Spanish meaning woollen material. Originally a square blanket with a hole for the head worn by people on horseback in, for example, Mexico.

11. Ballet: from French. Ballet was originally a French art form. Most of its vocabulary is therefore French: plié, arabesque, pas de deux, corps de ballet, etc.

12. Burkha: from Arabic meaning a heavy, loose garment which covers a woman's body entirely. She looks out through a small grille but the wearer herself is completely invisible. Worn in countries which practise an extreme form of Islam, most famously in Afghanistan under the Taleban. Spelling can vary.

Additional discussion

It is worth discussing with pupils why the English spelling of words such as 'tofu' and 'burkha' vary in English. It is because they come from languages which use a different alphabet, characters and or system from our familiar 26-letter European one. The word therefore passes into English initially as an oral/aural addition. Then, eventually when someone wants or needs to write the word, there is no agreed spelling so individuals take a phonetic stab at it and variants creep in. Take the Indian version of cottage cheese which now features on almost every Tandoori restaurant menu. I have seen it spelled 'paneer', 'panir', 'panur', 'panoir' and 'ponir'. Or consider the variations you see on CD cases of Peter Illyich Tchaikovsky's name.

>> Task 7.8

1a. Possibilities include:
   - viridescent
   - emerald
   - verdant
   - aquamarine

b. Possibilities include:
   - lemon
   - amber
   - gold
   - golden
   - mustard

2. As always, pupils will have their own ideas. These are just examples:

- Her **chalky** skin told me that Granny was really not very well.

- I think **ivory** walls will go well with the dark seasoned wooden doors in the sitting room.

- An animal that has no pigment in its skin is known as an **albino**.

3. As are these:

- Don't you put your **inky** fingers on my clean work!

- We once had a black cat named **'Sooty'**.

- The power failure which cut all the street lamps left us with **murky** darkness.

>> Task 7.9

More examples. Do make sure, one way or another, that pupils are on top of the spelling of these words once they've worked out ways of using them:

1. Britain grants asylum to refugees from troubled countries every year.

2. Sequined clothes seem to be making a fashion come-back, but all those tiny glittering discs are very fiddly to sew on.

3. It would be incongruous to meet the Queen by chance at a suburban railway station.

4. 'More pronouncements from the Head coming,' murmured Freddy as a cross-looking Mr Carr arrived in assembly.

5. We will go out for the day on Tuesday if the weather forecast is propitious.

6. Many of the prophecies made by George Orwell in his 1948 novel *Nineteen Eighty Four* have since come true.

7. While in the museum I admired the beautifully illustrated medieval Psalter which was open at Psalm 82.

8. My mother was planning to wear turquoise to the wedding but my aunt dissuaded her.

9. I enjoy the companionable silence that you get in our classroom when everyone's busy working.

10. The official started tapping the invalidation process into the computer because, following Ollie's bad behaviour, it had been decided to terminate his club membership and cancel his card.

Nuts and bolts

A rudimentary grasp of basic grammatical structure – the relationship between main and subordinate clauses and phrases is worth striving for because most pupils will make fewer mistakes if they can see a clear organisational pattern. It is also helpful, I think, if they learn to distinguish between clauses and phrases. Once this understanding is embedded they should be better equipped to be imaginative with grammar and to use, for example, sentence fragments in creative writing – as nearly all writers do for occasional effect. Look at the opening of Dickens's **Bleak House** for example.

And once pupils have absorbed the idea that complex sentences contain dependent clauses it is fairly simple to learn that compound sentences are merely simple sentences strung together with conjunctions like beads on a string – and that you should never use the expression 'simple sentence' to mean an easily understood sentence because 'simple' has a specific meaning in grammar.

>> Task 7.10

1. Back at Gemma's house, **I went into the sitting room** which was very large and untidy.
   I went into the sitting room.

2. I wondered, as I looked around me, **who had built the cathedral** which towered above us.
   I wondered who had built the cathedral.

3. **Our neighbour**, Elsie Smith, whom we try to help as much as we can, **is very elderly**.
   Our neighbour is very elderly.

4. **Carrots**, when they are braised, **peas**, freshly shelled, **and broccoli** which has been cooked in cheese sauce, **are my favourite vegetables**.
   Carrots, peas and broccoli are my favourite vegetables.

5. **Jess**, my cousin, **usually goes swimming with Louisa** who lives near her.
   Jess usually goes swimming with Louisa.

6. Wondering whom she should contact first, **my mother phoned Ben's parents** when he fell from our tree.
   My mother phoned Ben's parents.

>> Task 7.11

1. These are just examples, of course:
   - Roxana's house, which is much larger than ours, is in Park Avenue.
   - Once she had finished her homework, Lisa, always a conscientious girl, packed her school bag ready for the next day.
   - The River Thames, perhaps Britain's most famous river, rises in Gloucestershire, about 100 miles west of London.

- Readers of *English Year 9*, most of whom will be aged 13 or 14, are encouraged to read lots of books, especially the ones enjoyed by the author.

- As you carry it in, put the shopping on the table, which I have cleared ready for you.

2.
- E M Forster wrote *A Passage to India* but Rohinton Mistry wrote *A Fine Balance* and *The Jewel in the Crown* is by Paul Scott.

- We take the bus to school because we have bus passes and we like each other's company during the journey.

- I have been to India twice and to Australia once, but I have never been to America.

>> Task 7.12

1. 'Seventeen aircraft were sent on a mission tonight but none was lost,' announced the Second World War radio newsreader.

2. The lions sleep nearly all day.

3. The pride of lions sleeps nearly all day.

4. North Korea asks for help from other countries.

5. Everybody enjoys a good meal.

6. Neither of the men was found guilty at the end of the trial.

7. 'Has none of you heard of the Magna Carta?' demanded the exasperated history teacher.

8. Everyone in our class was distressed to hear the news.

9. The London Symphony Orchestra is playing an all Beethoven concert at Bridgwater Hall tonight.

10. There are two ways of spelling judgement or judgment: either is correct.

11. A splendid pack of timber wolves lives at Howlett's, the conservation zoo in Kent.

12. Italy is a longstanding member of the European Union.

>> Task 7.13

1. All members of the orchestra are eagerly looking forward to playing Beethoven's fifth symphony.

2. The orchestra is eagerly looking forward to playing Beethoven's fifth symphony

3. The pack of cards is on the table.

4. The class knows the school rules.

5. All the pupils know the school rules.

6. Each girl has a locker of her own.

7. All the girls have lockers of their own.

8. The zoo's new baby elephant was born to a herd which lives at Howlett's in Kent.

9. We have heard two versions of this event but neither is true.

10. Why is the team so scruffily dressed?

11. Why are team players so scruffily dressed?

12. Our local choir has lost its rehearsal space.

Additional passages

I agonised at length over which of these passages to include in English Year 9 *because it seems a distortion to read one without the other. The first explains (perhaps excuses) the second. In the end, for various reasons, I used neither so I'm very glad to have the opportunity to share them, chilling as they are, with you and your pupils now. When I have used these powerful pieces in class they have always engendered excellent discussion, some incredulity, and high level written work.*

The Indian Mutiny of 1857/58 ended the rule of the East India Company. Thereafter, India was ruled by the British Government. The 'mutiny', which many Indians regarded as a just revolution against an oppressor and occupier, was very bloody. On 15 July 1857, Nana Sahib, the native ruler at Cawnpore, massacred an entire garrison, including 200 women and children.

Later that month General Havelock, the Briton in charge of the relieving forces, described how he punished the perpetrators of the massacre.

Both these statements are, obviously, written from the British point of view.

A: Report of one of General Havelock's officers, dated 21 July 1857

I was directed to a house where all the poor miserable ladies had been murdered. It was alongside the Cawnpore Hotel, where Nana Sahib lived. I was never more horrified! The place was one mass of blood. I am not exaggerating when I tell you that the soles of my boots were more than covered with the blood of those poor wretched creatures. Portions of their dresses, collars, children's socks, and ladies' round hats lay round about, saturated with their blood; and in the sword-cuts on the pillars of the room long dark hair was carried by the edge of the weapon and there hung their tresses – a most painful sight! I have often wished that I had never been there, but sometimes wish that every soldier was taken there that he might witness the barbarities our poor countrywomen had suffered. Their bodies were afterwards dragged out and thrown down a well outside the building where their legs were to be seen sticking out in a mass of gory confusion ...

Those poor ladies were massacred on the 15th after we had thrashed the blackguards at the bridge. The collector, who gave the order for their death, was taken prisoner the day before yesterday and now hangs from a branch about 200 yards off the roadside. His death was, accidentally, a most painful one, for the rope was badly adjusted, and when he dropped, the noose closed over his jaw. His hands then got loose, and he caught hold of the rope and struggled to get free; but two men caught hold of his legs and jerked his body until his neck broke. This seems to me the just reward he should have got on earth for his barbarity.

B: General Havelock

Whenever a rebel is caught he is immediately tried, and unless he can prove a defence he is sentenced to be hanged at once; but the chief rebels or ringleaders I made first clean up a certain portion of the pool of blood, still two inches deep, in the shed where the fearful murder and mutilation of the women and children took place. To touch blood is most abhorrent to the high-caste natives, they think by doing so they doom their souls to perdition. Let them think so. My object is to inflict a fearful punishment for a revolting, cowardly, barbarous deed, and to strike terror into these rebels. The first I caught was a subahdar, or native officer, a high-caste Brahmin who tried to resist my order to clean up the very blood he had helped to shed; but I made the Provost-Marshal do his duty, and a few lashes soon made the miscreant accomplish his task. When done, he was taken out and immediately hanged, and after death buried in a ditch at the roadside. No one who has witnessed the scenes of murder, mutilation and massacre can ever listen to the word 'mercy' as applied to these fiends. The well of mutilated bodies – alas! containing upwards of 200 women and children – I have had decently covered in and built up as one large grave.

From the *Faber Book of Reportage* (Ed. John Carey), 1987

Discussion or comprehension points could include:
- horror of the massacre, what disturbed the writer most and why
- vindictiveness of General Havelock's reprisals and whether or not they were, by any standards, fair, just or reasonable
- how these incidents might have looked from an Indian perspective
- use of emotive language such as 'poor', 'miserable', 'blackguards', 'barbarity', 'rebel', 'miscreant', 'fiends'
- anything which can be inferred about the writers and the audience they are addressing.

Ageing is yet another eclectic and elastic topic and a good opportunity to discuss the ways in which different societies regard their older people. Many races and cultural groups are, for example, horrified by the British and American concept of institutions for old people in which they are housed and cared for when they can no longer look after themselves.

How many terms for, say, 'over-60s' can pupils think of? Old people, retired people, pensioners, OAPs, seniors, oldies, geriatrics, Ancient Britons, silver heads, grizzlies, wrinklies, etc. Get pupils to brainstorm and then discuss what the language itself – formal, accurate, affectionate, jokey, medical or whatever – tells you about context and the attitude of the speaker. Why are there so many different ways of referring to old people? What do we make of the fact that many of these terms are often used (or even coined) self-deprecatingly by the very people they refer to? Think about euphemisms too such as 'in the autumn of life', 'over the hill' and 'past one's prime'. How do they work?

What we mean by ageism and what we know about it is another good discussion topic. And all of this discussion work, of course, helps to lay the foundations for GCSE oral assessment.

From a text point of view there are many possibilities beyond the ones I included in *English Year 9*. The passages about Mr Collett in Jennifer Worth's *Shadows of the Workhouse* (2005 and republished as a Phoenix paperback in 2009) are, for example, deeply moving and beautifully written.

Do not forget the old people in Wordsworth's narrative poems such as 'Michael' or 'Simon Lee' either or Alan Bennett's 'A cream cracker under the settee'. The latter, written for Thora Hird (1911–2003), was one of Bennett's *Talking Heads* monologues first broadcast in 1987 and now widely available on DVD. *Talking Heads* is also published as a written text by BBC Books.

Then there's Sebastian Barry's splendid 2008 novel *The Secret Scripture* which was shortlisted for the 2008 Man Booker Prize and went on to win the 2009 Costa Prize. It tells the story of a very old lady in a nursing home in Ireland, details her tragic earlier life and explores her relationship with her doctor who, it turns out, is involved in her life in other ways, too.

You can also plunder the internet for obituaries of interesting old people such as Millvina Dean, last Titanic survivor, who died in May 2009. Or another recent fascinating one at the time of writing is Clement Freud, journalist, radio panellist, MP, advertiser of dog food, restaurateur – and renaissance man – who died in April 2009.

>> Task 8.1

1. A good answer might include some of these points:

- The 'Aged Parent' is profoundly deaf. He can hear nothing except the intensely loud nightly gunfire.

- He is in good general health: he feeds the fowls, heats the poker, seems alert, speaks sensibly – 'This is a fine place of my son's' – and is, apparently, left alone during the day to be self-sufficient, although he mostly sits by the fire and Pip perceives him as 'a very old man'.

- Wemmick is very fond of his father: '…his hard face really softened'.

- The old man is very proud of his son and his achievements. He tells Pip that he thinks the house should become a national monument after his son's death.

- Wemmick wants to give his father pleasure. That's why he asks Pip to keep nodding and why he organises the nightly 'treat' by firing the Stinger.

2. Wemmick:

- wants to keep his home life completely separate from his work

- forgets his home ('I leave the castle behind me') when he is in his office

- regards Mr Jaggers, his boss, as part of work and so has not told him about his old father or his home or invited him there

- is adamant that Pip should never mention Wemmick's home while he is in Wemmick's office: 'I don't want it professionally spoken about', in order to maintain this barrier.

3. A worthwhile discussion could lead to some of these points in a strong written response:

- Dickens, through Pip, is poking fun at Wemmick by referring to the tiny Walworth cottage as The Castle. That is how Wemmick and his father describe it and Pip goes along with it out of amused (incredulous?) respect.

- Wemmick has worked for 'a good many years' to create his little castle, complete with arbour in the garden and a battery. He now has it exactly as he wants it, although most people would regard the 'pitch' of it all as excessive. For Wemmick, however (and his father), perfection has been achieved. The alliterative 'p' heightens the humour here.

- Wemmick is very proud of his creation. Why else would he have invited Pip there? A great privilege, surely, since Wemmick is so keen that 'the office is one thing, and private life another'.

- The firing of the gun in the battery – as might happen in a real castle – using a red hot poker at the bottom would have been quite a complicated thing (and, rationally, completely pointless) to set up and develop. Yet the child-like Wemmick thinks it is fun and worthwhile and he knows his father loves it. He is like a miniature lord of the manor.

>> Task 8.2

1. Holroyd's aunt:

- is aware of her responsibilities – 'my aunt did her best' (line 19) although not very skilled at looking after a child

- is not always sensible or very grown up. She plays cricket with Holroyd in the dining room and sustains a fairly serious ('while we were waiting for the ambulance') head injury – presumably having been hit by a ball which she is less than adept at catching or hitting

- seems to be unmarried and living with her ageing parents as part of their household ('My aunt, my grandmother, Old Nan and myself')

- is, by inference, the stay-at-home sister of the author's more adventurous father who makes occasional visits with unsuitable gifts for his son.

2. A good answer might include some or all of these points, but this is not, of course, an exhaustive list and there are – as ever – other valid points which could be made:

- He is never allowed to feel a fully integrated member of the household. Even in adult life he remembers the repeated cry of 'What shall we do with the boy?' (line 1). He is, in this way reduced to the status of 'the boy' without a name.

- He seems to lack consistent, intelligent parenting. His father visits only very occasionally, briefly dashing in with 'a few flourishes and gestures' (lines 12/13) before leaving 'the fine tuning' (line 15) to his willing, but inept, aunt.

- He is aware that his grandparents, with their 'perpetual squabbling' (line 53) are not happy together so there is tension in the household.

- He has already suffered the breakdown of his parents' marriage.

- Once, he thinks about running away from Norhurst.

- On another occasion when he is in London he considers escaping to his grandparents' house which suggests he is unhappy in both places.

- No one – 'the family was baffled' (line 58) – seems to understand his needs or feelings.

3. Possible points of comparison include:

- Holroyd's grandfather is an independent householder featuring in a memoir, unlike the fictional Wemmick's father who is a dependent in his son's house. The former is much wealthier than the latter and lives nearly a century later.

- Wemmick's 'clean, cheerful comfortable' Aged Parent in Passage A seems very happy and contented unlike Holroyd's grandfather in Passage B who seems often to be distracted and angry 'blaming the government and all its works' (line 28) and 'looking worried from these days in London' (line 50).

- In Passage B, the deafness explains why the grandfather seems distant from his own household and grows ever more eccentric ('Part of his troubles arose from increasing deafness') – banging his head and sticking on more and more plasters or insisting on shaving in the lavatory. The deaf old man in passage A is affectionately characterised by his deafness which he and his son find imaginative ways of working round.

- Holroyd's grandfather finds his worsening deafness useful sometimes because it means he cannot hear, or take part in, arguments. Wemmick's father, too, makes the best of his condition gleefully looking forward to 'the Aged's treat'. The latter is much more childlike and much less curmudgeonly than the former.

4. This question is, obviously, wide open to a whole range of responses and would probably benefit from being discussed orally first. Or use it as an oral assignment rather than a written one. Humour, remember is very personal, although it is worth pointing out to pupils that you can see the humour in something and appreciate what a writer is trying – wryly, dryly, ironically, wittily, with understatement, alliteratively and so on – to do without necessarily finding it belly-laughingly funny yourself. There is a big spectrum from a quick inward grin to a guffaw. Points I would draw attention to include:

- Holroyd's sad but witty play on words and conventional cliché in Passage B: 'the double experience of my parents' marriage that had unhappily broken up and my grandparents' marriage that had unhappily been kept going' (lines 54/55).

- Dickens's repeated use – soon caught from Wemmick by Pip – of 'Aged Parent' and variations on it as a name for the old man. Repetition – and variations on a theme – is always a key element of comedy in Dickens.

- Holroyd's glorious (perhaps very English) understatement that 'we shouldn't have chosen the dining room to play cricket' (lines 21/22) which suddenly makes the child seem much older and wiser than the aunt.

- In Passage A the humorous pretentiousness of Wemmick's tiny 'castle' – in reality a cottage – with its battery and arbour.

- Holroyd's witty imagery in Passage B such as describing his grandfather's battered, plastered head as 'like the impasto of an expressionist painter' (line 30) or the dogs wisely slinking away from the irritated man (line 51).

>> Task 8.3

1. Of course there are as many ways of constructing a two-sentence summary of this obituary as there are pupils (and teachers) and there are no rights and wrongs. Try it yourself. Here's my effort:

- Polish-born Josef Stawinoga (1920–2007) lived 'rough' on a motorway reservation near Wolverhampton from 1967, when he last worked, until his death. Although he was well-known locally, often given food by Asian communities and his life style reluctantly condoned by the local council, nobody knows the truth about Mr Stawinoga's background which may have involved war activity.

2. Local folklore is the collection of stories which have grown up in the community around where he lives to explain Mr Stawinoga's background. Such stories are passed on from one person to another and no one knows where or how they started or how much truth there is in them. Examples include:

- service in the Polish army and detention as a Russian prisoner of war

- in self-imposed solitude on the rebound from a love affair

- punishing himself for a shameful war-time act.

3.   Look for some or all of the following points in a good answer. Mr Stawinoga:

- failed to pay the rent in nine lodging houses in the 1960s

- took to pushing all his belongings about in an old pram

- chose to live in a plastic tent on the central reservation of the A4150

- repeatedly refused offers of conventional housing

- occasionally took to the streets, sweeping with a brush

- became filthy with matted hair and a two foot long beard. When he died he had neither bathed nor showered for 30 years

- depended on local Asian religious groups for gifts of food to keep him going.

4.   This question is open to almost any sensible answer. If you discuss it with pupils first you might lead them towards some or all of these points as well as absorbing their ideas:

- People tend to admire eccentrics who stand out against the normal way of behaving (as long as it isn't hurting anyone). Hence the degree from Wolverhampton Polytechnic and the provision by the council of nine new tents over the years.

- There is a tradition in many religions of venerating hermits and other 'drop outs' as having an otherworldly, spiritual quality which must be supported. In the Christian religion, men and women, for instance those who became saints, were often very poor because they, like Mr Stawinoga, had rejected the clutter of life. Take St Jerome who lived for five years in the Syrian Desert in the fourth century or the sixth St Kentigern (Mungo) who raised himself as a hermit in the area which eventually became Glasgow. Hindus and Sikhs have similar traditions and respect for deliberately simple living. It comes down to a basic belief that worldly goods get in the way of spiritual development. So it is hardly surprising that local people came to regard Mr Stawinoga as a saintly figure and took him gifts of food. Bear in mind, too, that Wolverhampton has a massive Asian community so that Hinduism and Sikhism are statistically stronger there than Christianity. So perhaps it is not surprising that it was the Hindus and Sikhs who took him under their wing rather than the Christians. Or is it, more controversially, because church attenders tend to be rather conventional and disinclined to get involved with anything too messy too close to home?

- Many people are fascinated by characters and things about which there are unexplained mysteries. Witness the ongoing interest in the disappearance of Madeline McCann, Lord Lucan, the Loch Ness Monster, the *Mary Celeste*, and many more. Get pupils to brainstorm a list.

>> Task 8.4

1. Tithonus has been given what seemed to be a gift, but he is trapped. Immortality seems, on the face of it, a positive thing, but for him it is cruel. Rather than being a blessing, he is being, with strange irony, consumed by his unending life. It is a reversal of the norm in which it is death which, if personified, takes or 'consumes' a person. He watches with envy the woods which 'decay and fall', and the man who 'tills the fields and then lies beneath' because they are eaten by, or reabsorbed into the earth which produced them. But he, a 'grey shadow' which is 'marred and wasted', has only (personified) immortality which is, in its own cruel way, destroying him. He envies the 'happy men that have the power to die'.

2. Of course, pupils must be completely free to choose for themselves. It is entirely personal, but these are the ones I might choose if I were asked this question:

    ● 'my wrinkled feet' (line 65): it is the simple language here which makes for poignancy. Feet usually stay quite smooth into old age and wrinkles are associated with the face. So it is a way of stressing that Tithonus is already unnaturally old. It is a cold, stark image too which contrasts with the chilly beauty of Eos's glimmering thresholds and rosy shadows and highlights the tragedy of his knowing that 'thy nature can no longer mix with thine'.

    ● 'I wither slowly in thine arms' (line 6): 'Wither' is a very stark verb with the connotation of shrinking, disappearing and lessening. And for the speaker it's happening slowly as Tennyson stresses in this sentence in which all the vowels are long and mournful except for the feathery, whispered sound of 'wither'. The contrast reinforces the horror.

    ● 'left me maim'd' (line 20): maimed is a much more direct word than 'disabled' or 'handicapped'. Tennyson makes sure we hear it and appreciate its impact by alliteratively linking it with 'marred' in the previous line and using it to pre-echo the humming sound in the thrice repeated 'immortal' in the following two lines. The 'm' sound creates a hum of pain.

3. A good answer might notice that:

    ● Eos, with her light and ethereal 'ever-silent spaces of the East' (where dawn breaks) and 'far-folded mists', is contrasted with the 'wasted' Tithonus's 'wrinkled feet' and other very physical signs of his ageing.

    ● The silent goddess of the dawn, who travels on 'silver wheels' is often depicted in terms of light. She has 'gleaming halls', 'glimmering thresholds' and a cheek which 'begins to redden' as the sun rises.

    ● Tithonus, the narrator, is moved by thoughts of her 'pure brows', 'shoulders pure' and 'sweet eyes'.

    ● Tennyson also has Tithonus thinking about Eos's beautiful, disturbing weeping remembering 'thy tears are on my cheek'.

    ● Tennyson's account of the dawn as a team of horses leading Eos, which 'shake the darkness from their loosen'd manes, and beat the twilight into flakes of fire' is a dramatic account of Eos's beauty, too.

>> Task 8.5

1. A good answer might notice that the nursing home:

    - is staffed by doctors and nurses who make the residents sit up like children to eat with 'napkins in collars'

    - is unnaturally quiet and calm 'tidy and calm' with 'carpets, pressed to the walls, forbidding noise'

    - is odour free – 'no smell at all'. So keen are the staff to eliminate the 'smell of a hospital' that they have cut out good smells as well and the narrator longs for a strong, natural smell such as 'the scent/Of a hyacinth'

    - has only rather sterile, superficial conversation, too. Certain topics are not discussed. The 'language of death' for instance is not used

    - does not encourage residents to be individuals 'the men half-women and the women half-men'

    - ignores the past experience – pain ('tear-heavy handkerchiefs') or joy ('the pulse of love') – of the residents because 'this house has shut out the past'.

2. The residents:

    - are fed 'meals from the nursery' as if they were small children. They are 'dressed for a meal, napkins in collars'

    - have lost their sexual identity like very young children. 'The men have ceased to be men and the women, women'

    - have no choice over their lives. For example, 'except in anger, except in ignorance' they are discouraged from making a noise so that the place remains 'tidy and calm'

    - are being controlled by 'doctors' decisions' rather than treated as adults

    - are never reminded that time is passing or that death is approaching, because 'death/is an outcast here'.

3. The home has 'shut out the past'. It does not acknowledge that behind these 'wrinkled faces' is a lifetime of human experience, including 'The family increase and birth's harvesting'. At the same time, 'it dare not face the future' because all that lies ahead is death and that 'is shut from this house'. So all that is left is the present and because it is so shallow and empty it is dangerous, because it strands the narrator in a non-existent place with which she cannot cope. 'I who am very young here feel part-guilty/part helpless'. For her the present is part of the past and the future so she cannot communicate with the residents. She feels 'out of place'. So for her and for the residents the 'perilous present' is very bleak.

4. This is a very wide-ranging and quite challenging assignment. Before long, as pupils embark on public examination courses, they will have to write textual comparison essays. Here I try to get them started in a supportive way. Discussion is always a good idea first and, by now, if pupils have worked through Task 8.4 and the rest of Task 8.5 they should have a fair working knowledge of the two poems. Some pointers which might help:

- Tithonus in Passage D is experiencing extreme old age and observing it in himself. The narrator of Passage E is an outsider reflecting on a group of old people. There is no individual focus in Passage E – partly to stress that the way in which the residents are treated.

- Passage D is rooted in a Greek Myth. Passage E takes as its starting point a very ordinary twenty-first century experience – visiting a nursing home. And they were written over 100 years apart. Nonetheless some of the vocabulary is the same. The word 'wrinkled', for example, occurs in both poems.

- Passage D is written in iambic pentameter and blank verse. This gives it the same impassioned rhythm flow you find in many of Shakespeare's great passages. Passage E is also blank verse, but line length and metre are freer which gives it a more reflective tone.

- Both poems use patterning. For example, there is a fair amount of repetition of phrases, sometimes inverted in Passage E 'men half-women, the women half-men' which conveys a sense of dreamy half consciousness like that of the residents. Tennyson's alliteration in Passage D ('yearning for thy yoke', 'Release me, and restore me') helps to underpin Tithonus's desperate, fluent rhetoric and firm monosyllabic, hammer blow lines, like 'Time is a scheme of light and dark', helps to make the stark realisation of the resident's position very clear. Death is coming for them very soon in 'a night, an hour, for how long?' – but for Tithonus in Passage D there is only a future of perpetual ageing.

➤➤ Task 8.6

There is, of course, no set way of writing a summary but this is the sort of thing I would encourage pupils to aim for – even shrinkage and all the main points but without fussy detail:

- Gerald Berkowitz is disappointed with this production of King Lear which he finds generally unoriginal, ordinary and with little to add to our understanding of the play. For him the best part was the second half in which Ian McKellen as Lear is very moving although he is unimpressive in the first half. Apart from William Gaunt as Gloucester and, occasionally Ben Meyjes as Edgar, Berkowitz thinks all the other supporting roles are competently, but uninspiringly, played and he dislikes the opening.

Writing about literature

This is an opportunity for pupils to study a short passage of (non-fiction) prose and to work out how they might write about it. Generally, pupils find close reading and textual analysis of prose harder than poetry.

Here is another example to share with them, also based on an extract from Passage C.

Josef Stawinoga, who died on 28 October, aged 86, was a hermit who lived for nearly forty years in a tent on the central reservation of the A4150 Wolverhampton inner ring road – between PC World and a bathroom showroom.

Because this is the obituary's opening statement it has to summarise the facts and answer the questions who (Josef Stawinoga), what (died) and when (28 October). It also gives his age and the most interesting thing about him, for which he is famous: that he lived on a main road reservation for four decades. This is a pretty standard format with which to start an obituary. In order to keep it brief and to-the-point, the obituarist has used two parenthetical dependent clauses 'who died on October 28th' and 'who lived for nearly forty years in a tent on the central reservation of the A4150 Wolverhampton inner ring road' and two subordinate phrases 'aged 86' and '– between PC World and a bathroom showroom'. All this hangs on the main, interrupted clause 'Josef Stawinoga … was a hermit'. It is a very clear means of expression.

The final phrase is not strictly necessary but it highlights the strangeness of Mr Stawinoga's choosing to live where he did and it is affectionately humorous. The vocabulary is direct with 'hermit', 'tent', 'died', 'lived', and so on. Only adjectives which are necessary to the sense such as 'central', 'inner', 'ring' and 'bathroom' are included. Otherwise the sentence relies mostly on strong nouns and verbs. The result is a sentence which flows smoothly and communicates its meaning with elegance.

>> Task 8.8

I don't think you can ever do too much work on the meaning and origin or words – which most pupils find quite interesting anyway. I would always encourage them to make the notes for this task in any way which they think helps them. My suggestions here are only examples:

- panorama: a view of a wide – or all encompassing scene. Long, whole-school photographs in which the camera pivots are known as panoramic photographs

- arboretum: a scientific collection of living trees. Winkworth Arboretum is a famous one in Surrey

- pandemic: a very wide, global-spreading disease. Much worse than an epidemic

- demonise: to treat someone or something as if he/she/it were devilish. For example, smoking has been demonised in Europe in recent years

- arborist: specialist in the cultivation of trees. Might be employed in a nursery or by the Forestry Commission

- panacea: a wide-ranging cure. Now usually used as a metaphor. The provision of litter bins, for instance, is not a panacea for the sort of people who will throw litter on the ground anyway

- aborescent: having the shape or characteristics of a tree. The drive leading to the house was lined with aborescent sculptures

- panoply: complete array. Originally all the equipment of a warrior. We gazed at the panoply of Christmas lights festooning the house

- aboreal: tree-living. For example, squirrels are aboreal animals

- demonic: possessed by demons or devils or seeming to be. Demonic laughter, for example.

>> Task 8.9

More examples. Let the pupils be as creative as they wish:

1. It is hard to bestir yourself in the morning when it's cold outside but warm in bed.

2. Central Italy was devastated by the loss of life and infrastructure in the 2009 earthquake.

3. We need continuous internet access because it is difficult to communicate when the connection is intermittent.

4. The Beatles revered the guru they consulted in India.

5. 'I saw the burglar running away down the path,' attested Amelia when questioned in court by the defence counsel.

6. I feel very guilty about not having helped the old man next door who has now died so, as penance, I shall do some voluntary work.

7. Most religions involve paying homage to some sort of god or gods.

8. Although my aunt was badly concussed in the accident she was still lucid enough to be able tell us what had happened.

9. He set off towards the river carrying all the accoutrements for a day's fishing including lines, seat, umbrella, bucket, bait and a packed lunch.

10. The straits of Malacca are notoriously perilous because many pirates operate there.

11. Any elderly person who is finding life difficult deserves to be treated with compassion.

12. 'Yes, but get to the point and tell us what you saw,' interpolated Anna impatiently.

13. 'The fault must be inherent,' said the telephone engineer, 'because I can find no obvious reason for your problem.'

14. Teachers must learn to differentiate between pupils who learn in different ways.

15. The slender, gnarled trunks of the vines were twisted along the vineyard's support wires.

Nuts and bolts

Clause analysis, as such, is right out of fashion. Nonetheless I think, without labouring it too much, that it is valuable for pupils to have basic knowledge of how complex sentences are constructed for (at least) two reasons.

First, awareness will help to inform the structure of their own sentences so they can write using conventional grammar when it is called for and, in creative context, break the 'rules' with confidence when they need or want to.

Second, it is invaluable underpinning for the analytical work required by AS and A2 English Language and English Language and Literature. And, in my experience, the earlier you bed in this learning the more readily it is absorbed. Keep using the terms too when you are studying text so that the pupils acquire real 'ownership'.

I have set the basics out as clearly and simply as I can on pages 155 to 156.

Task 8.10

Pupils learn, of course, by applying and consolidating what they have just learned. As usual these are just examples:

1. Manner:

   Joss laid the table for dinner **as he always did at around 7 p.m.** (adverbial clause)

   Joss always laid the table for dinner **at around 7 p.m.** (adverbial phrase)

   The ducks waddled **as if they were in a great hurry**. (adverbial clause)

   The ducks waddled **very quickly**. (adverbial phrase)

2. Place:

   Where there are mountains you usually find lakes. (adverbial clause)

   You usually find lakes **in mountainous areas**. (adverbial phrase)

   Deepa sat on the bench **where Eve was already sitting**. (adverbial clause)

   Deepa sat on the bench **beside Eve**. (adverbial phrase)

3. Reason:

   As the rain has been so heavy we are staying indoors. (adverbial clause)

   We are staying indoors **because of heavy rain**. (adverbial phrase)

   My grandparents have moved house **because they wanted to live nearer to us**. (adverbial clause)

   My grandparents have moved to a house **nearer to us**. (adverbial phrase)

4. Time:

Once I have finished *David Copperfield* I shall read *Dombey and Son*. (adverbial clause)

I shall read *Dombey and Son* **after** *David Copperfield*. (adverbial phrase)

When I leave school I shall go to university. (adverbial clause)

I shall go to university in **four years' time**. (adverbial phrase)

>> Task 8.11

More practice and more examples of colons and semi-colons in use – in case your creativity is running dry:

- Mark Antony, a wily politician in Shakespeare's *Julius Caesar*, begins his famous funeral oration with these words: 'Friends, Romans, countrymen, lend me your ears.'

- Try this: swim 50 lengths before breakfast.

- The enquiry found that: (a) there was no case to answer and (b) that Mrs Jessop had been maligned.

- The following people were present: Mum, Dad, Grandpa, Auntie Sylvia and my cousins, Sam and Harry.

- We called at house after house; we sang in courtyards and porches, outside windows or in the damp gloom of hallways; we heard voices from hidden rooms; we smelt rich clothes and strange hot foods; we saw maids bearing in dishes or carrying away coffee cups; we received nuts, cakes, figs, preserved ginger, dates, cough drops and money but we never once saw our patrons.

- While you're in the supermarket please buy: some bananas and get plenty, because we all like them and there are none left in the fruit bowl; a large piece of strong cheddar cheese, which we can use in tomorrow's cheese and potato pie when there will be six people for a quick lunch before the tennis match; salad for six people but don't forget that Freddie can't stand radishes; two large bottles of mineral water as the forecast is for a hot spell and some pretty paper napkins to save washing cloth ones when we're busy.

- A garden shed is a building; York Minster is a piece of architecture.

- There are many breeds of dog; the chihuahua is the smallest.

- The reasonable man adapts himself to the world; the unreasonable man persists in trying to adapt the world to himself.

> Note too, the use of semi-colons in the passage from *Emma*, below. And there's a nice colon in line 40 in Passage C in *English Year 9*, page 145.

Additional passage

Jane Austen's Emma, *published in 1816 is surely one of the most gloriously witty and well observed of her six novels – although it's hard to fault any of them. Who could ever forget the appalling Mrs Elton or poor little Harriet Smith whom the better-born Emma – with such a lot to learn – manipulates so thoughtlessly. And as for Mr Woodhouse: he must be one of the most tiresome elderly characters in fiction. Great fun to read about but thank goodness he isn't my responsibility. This passage comes from the beginning of the novel in which Austen begins to show and tell us what Mr Woodhouse is really like. Miss Taylor, governess, companion to the motherless Emma and very much part of the Woodhouse family has just married Mr Weston. Pupils are often surprised at how easy Austen is to read so you might use this passage as a lever to launch them into* Emma.

She dearly loved her father, but he was no companion for her. He could not meet her in conversation, rational or playful.

The evil of the actual disparity in their ages (and Mr Woodhouse had not married early) was much increased by his constitution and habits; for having been a valetudinarian all his life, without activity of mind or body, he was a much older man in ways than in years; and although everywhere beloved for the friendliness of his heart and his amiable temper, his talents could not have recommended him at any time.

Her sister, though comparatively but little removed by matrimony, being settled in London, only sixteen miles off, was much beyond her daily reach; and many a long October and November evening must be struggled through at Hartfield, before Christmas brought the next visit from Isabella and her husband and their little children to fill the house and give her pleasant society again.

Highbury, the large and populous village almost amounting to a town, to which Hartfield, in spite of its separate lawn and shrubberies and name, did really belong, afforded her no equals. The Woodhouses were in first consequence there. All looked up to them. She had many acquaintance in the place, for her father was universally civil, but not one among them could be accepted in lieu of Miss Taylor for even half a day. It was a melancholy change; and Emma could not but sigh over it and wish for impossible things, till her father awoke, and made it necessary to be cheerful. Her spirits required support. He was a nervous man, easily depressed; fond of every body that he was used to, and hating to part with them; hating change of any kind. Matrimony, as the origin of change, was always disagreeable; and he was by no means yet reconciled to his own daughters marrying, nor could he ever speak of her but with compassion, though he was now obliged to part with Miss Taylor too; and from his habits of gentle selfishness and of being never able to suppose that other people could feel differently from himself, he was very much disposed to think Miss Taylor had done as sad a thing for herself as for them, and would have been a great deal happier if she had spent all the rest of her life at Hartfield. Emma smiled and chatted as cheerfully as she could, to keep him from such thoughts; but when tea came, it was impossible for him not to say exactly as he had said at dinner,

'Poor Miss Taylor! – I wish she were here again. What a pity it is that Mr Weston ever thought of her!'

From *Emma* by Jane Austen (1816).

Discussion or comprehension points could include:

- character of Mr Woodhouse

- authorial voice

- what Austen means by 'first in consequence there'

- Emma's implied feelings about her father and living alone with him

- what we learn about the rest of the Woodhouse family

- attitudes to aging.

Although the passages in this chapter mostly relate to science – Alexander Fleming, Marie Curie, Archimedes – I tried also to widen the concept so that a 'eureka moment' is associated with discovery in general rather than limiting it to pure science. That's how Wordsworth's wonderful blank verse account of crossing the Alps got in. Both Passage E ('Dissection' by Colin Rowbotham) and Passage F (from *The Time Machine* by H G Wells) start with science but are actually about other kinds of discovery. So, one way and another, there's a lot there.

If you're looking for other avenues along which to explore this subject further then there's the whole genre of science fiction – written pretty continuously since H G Wells and Jules Verne. I think John Wyndham's *The Chrysalids* (1955) is my favourite science fiction novel of all time. Or if you want to go further back don't forget Mary Shelley's *Frankenstein* (1818).

Have a look at *Genesis* by Bernard Beckett (2009), too. Aimed at very able young readers it is set in a physically sealed-off republic in what we know as New Zealand and it overtly explores – with intelligent elegance – life's big mysteries such as what makes us human, the role of altruism, the use of history and the danger of knowledge.

Encourage pupils to access the *Oxford Dictionary of National Biography*. Biographies of Newton, Faraday, Darwin and hundreds of others are there waiting for them.

Another good source of eureka! material is newspapers which report scientific discoveries and breakthroughs – especially medical ones – almost daily. I might, for example, ask a Year 9 class to scour newspapers for, say a month. Then get them to bring in one chosen cutting dealing with a scientific matter which they have two minutes to present to the class. Or, if you (or they) prefer, they could research online versions of newspapers and use the electronic white board for the presentation. Either way, it would broaden the base of scientific reading and incorporate some valuable oral work and GCSE preparation at the same time.

>> Task 9.1

1. There is obviously no one way of doing this but a good attempt might look something like this:

   - Alexander Fleming (1881–1955) was a Scot who trained as a doctor but worked in research.

   - He noticed – a chance discovery – mould inhibiting bacteria in 1928.

   - His observation led to the development of antibiotics.

   - He became very famous and was awarded many honours.

2. These are the main points to look for:

   - Fleming was studying the germ which causes septic infections.

   - He was writing a chapter for a bacteriology journal.

   - He went on holiday so things were left lying about in his laboratory.

- There was a plate culture of bacteria which had not been thrown away.

- It had gone mouldy.

- Where there was mould on the dish there were no bacteria.

- Although his colleagues were initially unimpressed, Fleming thought he was on to something.

- So he worked on the mould Penicillium notatum, a common strain which he thought had got into the laboratory via the open window, and its 'juice', for the next six months.

- The inference is that he reasoned that if this mould could kill germs in a lab it could, perhaps, be used to treat septic infections, too.

- Although he presented his findings at two science conferences in 1929, for various reasons it was more than ten years before it took off.

3. Fleming was the son of a Scottish farmer who died when the boy was seven. He had three siblings and four half-siblings from his father's first marriage. He married Sareen who died in 1949. His second wife was Amalia Vourekas whose maiden name was Coutsouri. She was a work colleague whom he had known since 1946. They married in 1953, two years before Fleming's death.

4. This is quite complicated and pupils will probably need to read the relevant section of the passage several times to work out what actually happened. It boils down to something along these lines:

- Another group of scientists (in Oxford) began experimenting with penicillin in 1940 and published their results.

- Interested, Fleming visited to find out what they were doing.

- He thought they had stolen his work without crediting him.

- He wrote in medical journals criticising the Oxford scientists.

- He also spoke about this publicly, describing his discovery in 1928 and his painstaking work during the 1930s.

- Then the rest of the press picked up the story.

- That, suddenly, gave penicillin and its potential a very high profile. Fleming was given many honours and became famous.

>> Task 9.2

1. These seem to me to be the main deducible points:

- born Poland

- wife of Pierre Curie

- lived in France

- discovered radioactive radium and polonium with her husband

- joint (with husband) Nobel Prize winner
- two children – Irene and Eve
- widowed by road accident in 1906
- much publicised affair with Paul Langevin, a married man, after Pierre's death
- toured America with daughters in 1921
- nursed by Eve, who lived with her, during final illness
- died of leukaemia 1934.

2a. Eve differed from the other Curies in that she:
- did not personally win a Nobel Prize (as her sister and parents did)
- was not a professional scientist
- wrote books including a famous biography of her mother
- had a career as a concert pianist
- became a war correspondent, journalist, charity director and publisher in the second half of her life
- lived latterly in Greece and the USA as well as in Paris and became an American citizen aged 56
- lived to be over 100.

b. In common with the other Curies, Eve:
- was a high achiever
- studied science initially and had a degree in it
- married, as her mother and sister had.

3. There is a great deal which could be said here. Encourage detailed discussion but make sure pupils don't miss these key points:

- The opening of Passage A is a very dry, detailed – almost tortuously formulaic – account of the family Fleming was born into. The opening of Passage B is a clear 36-word, succinct summary of Eve Curie's claim to fame. Like most newspaper articles it gives you the essence of everything which is to follow like an expanded headline.

- Many of the sentences in Passage A are quite long and complex with a fair amount of technical and scientific vocabulary, such as 'Fleming was studying colony variation in the staphylococcus, the germ that causes septic infections, for a chapter he was writing for the *System of Bacteriology*' (lines 29–31). It was almost certainly written by a scientist although the meaning is made clear. In Passage B, the language is less scientific (although we still get 'synthesis of radioactive elements'). Both passages occasionally use very simple, factual sentences such as 'They eventually married on 9 April 1955' (Passage A, lines 83/84) and 'She became an American citizen in 1958' (Passage B, line 67).

- Passage B seems easier to read than Passage A because the text seems less dense. This is partly because – another newspaper technique – Passage B uses quite short paragraphs. Most consist of only two or three sentences and several are single-sentence paragraphs. Almost all the paragraphs in Passage A are quite long and involved and contain detailed strings of sentences. This is a rather more traditional way of writing – closer, say, to Dickens or Austen than most modern novelists.

- So factual is Passage A that at line 72 it gives Fleming's honours as a colon-preceded list without attempt at stylistic elegance. In comparison Passage B is much more literary and fluid. After line 50, for example, it gives us a list of the work Eve Curie did after the war but it is presented as a series of paragraphs, each one shaped in a different way grammatically, so that it doesn't feel repetitive.

- Passage B includes more personal information than Passage A. We hear about Eve Curie's sister, her mother's affair, her 'attractive, chic and dark-haired' appearance, her relationship with her mother and her marriage. Apart from the bare facts about his parents and siblings and the names of his two wives there is almost nothing personal in Passage A about Fleming apart from his work habits and what we can infer about him from his reaction to the Oxford group's attitude to what he regarded as 'his' juice.

- Passage A tells its story in a chronological, step-by-step way ending with Fleming's death and cremation in the final paragraph. Passage B unwinds its story in a more convoluted way. We don't get the account of Eve Curie's birth, for instance, until line 40. The key facts about her life come first – which is usual in an obituary. Eve Curie's death is reported in the first sentence because it has only just happened. In that sense, an obituary also serves as a news item.

>> Task 9.3

1. A good answer will include some or all of these points. Archimedes:

   - observed that when you get into a bath of water the water level rises

   - worked out that if you fill something to the brim with water and then immerse an object in it the volume of the water displaced is equal to the volume of the immersed objects

   - realised he could use this way of measuring the volume of an awkward item such Hieron II's wreath

   - began to understand that water pressure makes objects and bodies lighter in water

   - perhaps solved the mystery of why some things float but others sink.

2. A mini-biography of Archimedes based on this passage might note that he:

   - was an Ancient Greek scientist

   - was born in Syracuse, Sicily c. 290 BC

   - was a member of the royal family and therefore rich enough not to have to work

- spent much time reflecting on mathematics and mechanics
- was, in effect, a science advisor to King Heiron II
- in old age designed ships, catapults and, possibly, fire-directing mirrors to help during the attack on Syracuse by the Romans
- was killed in 211 BC in Syracuse by rampaging Roman soldiers.

3. There is a good deal to discuss here, building on the work already done for Tasks 9.1 and 9.2. Points to note about Passage C include:

- The vocabulary is as simple and un-technical as possible – 'float', 'sink', 'problems', 'upward push', etc. When they are unavoidable, scientific words such as 'density' are explained within the text (lines 21/22).

- The writer opens with a direct question to the reader as a teacher would, and assumes that the reader is unlikely to know the answer because he or she is still a child. So the text is directly didactic – but it never uses that sort of adult vocabulary.

- Archimedes's discoveries are partly fictionalised and told in the form of a story. 'One day …' (line 26) and 'When Archimedes was an old man…' (line 50).

- On the other hand it makes it clear that there is a lot about Archimedes which we don't know for certain. 'Archimedes may also…' (line 30), '…probably didn't do this' (line 37), 'This probably didn't happen' (line 47). In that sense it is good non-fiction writing which doesn't pretend that things are established facts when they are not.

- The story runs chronologically and straightforwardly from Archimedes's birth to his death (unlike both Passages A and B) so that it is easy for a child to follow.

- The story is told visually – as if it were something we were watching on film. First we see Archimedes puzzling over how to measure the wreath's volume. Then he reflects while he is bathing. Later, we imagine him working on his ships and weapons and visualise his brutal death at the hand of a Roman soldier. Children usually relate to visual images most easily.

- Sentences and paragraphs are quite short. The paragraph which begins at line 38, for instance, contains five succinct sentences, one of which consists of only two words ('They sink', line 43). This style is accessible for young-ish children, some of whom might otherwise get lost in long, convoluted sentences such the ones sometimes used in Passage A.

- The passage assumes that the child reader will have some idea of what we mean by weight and volume, but not necessarily how they relate to each other. So it builds on what children know and their own experience such as how water behaves when you immerse objects in it. It is carefully targeted to a reading and science age somewhere around 9 years old.

- The piece has some entertainment value as a story because we imagine Archimedes beavering away helping Hieron – perhaps running naked through the streets in excitement – and then dying violently and dramatically after a long life (he was about 79 when he died) working on the things which interested him. It is a satisfying tale with a beginning, middle and an end. It is also quite dramatic.

>> Task 9.4

1. Wordsworth is surprisingly easy to read but difficult to understand because, of course, his trademark was complex, pantheistic philosophy expressed in everyday language. Some or all of these points might be in a good answer and thoughtful pupils may come up with others.

   Wordsworth (and it really is him this time not a 'narrator' since this is an autobiography) feels:

   - temporarily overwhelmed or 'lost in a cloud'
   - awed: 'Power,/in all the might of its endowments, came/athwart me', (lines 40–42)
   - aware of the glory of the human soul and human imagination (lines 4–5) because the crossing has made him rejoice
   - closer to God or 'the invisible world' where 'Greatness make abode'
   - very small in comparison with the vastness of nature (the Alps) and the fact that everything ('our destiny, our nature') which makes a human being will not last long except hope which 'can never die'
   - conscious of his own thoughts: 'The mind…/thinks not of'
   - joyful: 'access of joy'.

2. The men in Wordsworth's group:

   - stop trudging, regain their motivation, and 'hurried fast' downhill
   - follow the road which previously they 'had miss'd' into a narrow 'gloomy' valley
   - continue for several hours along the line of a 'brook and road' with 'fellow travellers'
   - notice the treeline, waterfalls, and 'black drizzling crags' above them

3. These would be my choices but, naturally, this question is freely open to any answer. The important thing is to encourage pupils to justify their choices fully:

   - 'different dejection' (line 4): suggests a thoughtful, reflective sadness. The choice of two alliterative polysyllables gives the temporary low-level ('an under-thirst') unhappiness a rueful sense of his not quite understanding why he felt as he did.

   - 'like the overflowing Nile' (line 61): stresses the extent to which Wordsworth is overcome by the joy he feels. He rarely uses simile or resorts to hyperbole so it is all the more striking and effective when he does. It is faintly incongruous too. Although, like the Alps, the Nile is an awe-inspiring natural phenomenon, it is hot and muddy and very different from the 'thwarting winds, bewildered and forlorn' (line 73) of the Alps.

   - 'giddy prospect of the raving stream' (line 77): is a colourful piece of imagery which personifies the rapidly flowing stream as someone who is 'giddy' or 'raving'. There is also a suggestion that anyone looking at the stream 'giddy prospect' will be thrown off balance, too.

>> Task 9.5

1. Things which surprise the narrator about his rat include:

    - yellowness reminds him of marzipan

    - under the 'damp, yellow fur' is the 'taut, elastic' body wall, 'a sack that is fat with innards' (line 20)

    - the organs are very neatly packed 'a firmly coiled discipline/of overlapping liver, folded gut' (lines 26/27)

    - there is no 'oozing mash' (line 25) or the 'blood/or the yellow juices' (line 9) he expects

    - it reminds him of a small machine, such as a clock, but nothing will ever make it tick again

    - it is different from the diagram in the book

    - it is harder to peg out than he expects because the 'pins are twisted and the board is hard'.

> Note: although it isn't strictly relevant to this question I would also, at some point in the discussion of this poem, draw attention to the word 'crucify' and its connotations. It carries resigned sympathy for the rat and a sense of awe that 'the victim' has to be forcefully laid out in a cross shape which has echoes of Jesus and the treatment of common criminals in the Roman Empire – but this rat is completely innocent. It also confers power, perhaps unsought for, on the narrator who is controlling the rat, although he in turn is merely doing what he is told to do in his science lesson. You could argue that just as an ordinary Roman soldier doing a job was a mere intermediary between the Empire and the condemned man, so the narrator of the poem is just an intermediary between the rat and the force of science education – but that may be carrying the analogy too far.

2. He reflects on 'what it is that has left this rat' (line 29). All the rat's organs are there and perfect. But that indefinable life force has gone. The machine has stopped and 'a month of probing could not make it go again' (line 30). So he is asking himself what life and death really are.

    At the same time there are the everyday facts of school life to which he switches quite abruptly:

    - the bell

    - packing the rat away

    - hand washing

    - lunch.

    It is incongruous that he should be thinking about the essence of life and death one minute and eating a meat pie the next, but by knitting these details together

Rowbotham makes it clear that the narrator's education is ongoing at several levels. He is learning about the anatomy and physiology of the machine-like rat as well as pondering metaphysical questions – all within the constraints of a conventional school timetable. He is a resilient schoolboy who doesn't lose himself in metaphysics for long.

3. This question is probably best discussed before a written answer is attempted. Points of comparison I would steer pupils towards thinking about include:

    - Wordsworth is marvelling at the grandeur of the Alps while Rowbotham's narrator is struck by the intricacy and perfection of the rat's organs. Both react with awe.

    - Both are interested in their own reaction to the experience rather than stopping at the experience itself. Wordsworth in Passage D mentions 'The mind beneath such banners militant' (line 56) and Rowbotham in Passage E stresses his own wonderment.

    - Both are first person accounts. Passage D is autobiographical. We know Wordsworth really did cross the Alps and wrote about it afterwards. Rowbotham himself is not necessarily the speaker in Passage E, although the sense of immediacy is as strong as Wordsworth's.

    - Both passages use rhythm for effect. Wordsworth's iambic pentameters are fairly steady (and reinforce the sense of the walking onward) except where he deliberately breaks the rhythm for dramatic effect such as at line 38. Rowbotham's freer, more uneven verse relies on the jagged rhythm to evoke the narrator's actions and thoughts which are not smooth. In other words, both poems are patterned but Passage E is irregular.

›› Task 9.6

1. Look for some or all of these points. The exquisite creatures:

    - are small in stature – about four feet tall (line 57)

    - speak a 'strange and very sweet' (line 68) or 'cooing' (line 91) language

    - are pretty, graceful and apparently frail like Dresden china (line 84)

    - have faces with small ears, tiny ears, thin-lipped red mouths, pointed chins and large eyes (lines 86/87)

    - have small, soft tentacle-like hands (line 73)

    - have jaw-line length curly hair on their heads but no facial hair (lines 84–86)

    - wear tunics and sandals (lines 58 and 94).

They disappoint the narrator because they do not seem to be intellectually advanced. They use gestures to ask him whether a thunderstorm had brought him from the sun as if they were 'fools'. He had assumed that if you travel 800 millennia forward in time you will find things have progressed. Instead, these people remind him of five-year-old children.

2. The narrator is discovering, among other things:

    ● a new world in the year 802,000

    ● that it has a built environment consisting of statues, parapets, columns and buildings

    ● a diminutive people who speak a strange language and who seem to lack scientific knowledge

    ● that he has the machine, but it is not always predictable or controllable. He has difficulty landing in this time (lines 44–49)

    ● that the passage of time doesn't necessarily mean what he views as progress.

3. I would discuss this orally with the group before (or perhaps instead of) asking pupils to write an answer. Starting points for discussion include:

    ● Wells's description of the built environment could be a modern or medieval Middle Eastern city.

    ● The people are strangely lacking in fear – which suggests lack of experience – as well as being scientifically naïve as if they have 'lost' the discoveries of the first and second millennia. Learning isn't always continually cumulative.

    More generally:

    ● We are often told by scientists that human beings are getting larger with each generation (because of better food, housing and so on) so is it likely that in 800,000 years time they could be much smaller?

    ● If so what has happened to change things in the intervening 800 millennia?

    ● Is it possible or likely that over 800 millennia the dominant (perhaps human) group on earth will have several endings and beginnings and so develop in an unimagined direction?

Writing about literature

Here is another example to share with pupils, this time based on two and a half lines of 'The Prelude' (Passage D, lines 14–16):

Ere long we follow'd
Descending by the beaten road that led
Right to the rivulet's edge and then broke off.

Wordsworth stresses the rather lugubrious plod of this walk (at this point they seem to be lost) with the heavy monosyllable of 'Ere long we' underpinned by the long vowel sounds of 'ere', 'we' and the second syllable of 'follow'd'. The rhythm then speeds up in the perfect symmetry of the iambic pentameter – 'Des**cend**ing **by** the **beat**en **road** that **led**' helped by the alliterative 'b' as they plod downhill towards the 'rivulet' whose moving water you can hear in the ripplingly alliterative 'r'. At the end of the sentence comes a return to the flat monosyllables of disappointment; 'and then broke off' as the road ends.

Writing tip

It is usually quite a challenge to persuade young writers to part with their gratuitous adverbs since they've been told (misguidedly in my view) almost since they could hold a pencil that modifiers such as adjectives and adverbs ('describing words') make your writing more interesting. And yet some of the finest writers – Orwell, Hemingway, Camus, Achebe, for example – use very few.

One of my particular bugbears is '**clutter adverbs**' which add nothing to meaning and detract from incisiveness. Why say 'I sincerely believe…' when the elegant and plain 'I believe' is stronger? Some will argue that adverbs such as 'really', 'absolutely', and so on are used for emphasis but I think they have the reverse effect. And as for the almost universally misused 'hopefully'…!

Sometimes, as an exercise to teach this point I have given pupils a passage full of expendable adverbs and asked them to write an edited version from which most of the adverbs are removed. Then you can discuss with them which is the better version and why.

This is part of a genuine letter I once received and I find it works well for this purpose.

Dear Mrs Elkin

Thank you for your letter dated 17th April which I actually received on 24th. I am extremely sorry that you have had to wait so long for an answer.

We sadly note your problems with our product but we are extremely grateful to you for kindly drawing the matter to our attention.

We will definitely look carefully at the fault to see if we can, hopefully, find a way of making sure this doesn't happen again.

Meanwhile I enclose a gift voucher which I sincerely hope will help to compensate you for your trouble.

Yours sincerely

>> Task 9.9

Definitions will be thoughtful (I hope) but look for his sort of thing:

1. Homonym: one of a group of words which have different meanings but which are spelt or pronounced the same, such as meat/meet/mete, stake/steak (different meanings, same pronunciation) or boot (spelt and pronounced the same whether it's part of a car or footwear) or rose (spelt and pronounced the same whether it's a flower or the past tense of the verb 'to rise').

2. Toponym: a place name, such as Redhill, Chesterfield, Lancashire, East Anglia, Dover or England.

3. Synonym: one of a group of words which are similar in meaning. King, monarch, sovereign, ruler and emperor are synonyms. So are seize, grab, snatch and take.

4. Eponym: a word derived from a person's name. For example, the word 'sandwich' comes from the 4th Earl of Sandwich (1718–92) who is supposed to have invented the idea. The verb 'to boycott' comes from an action by Charles Cunningham Boycott (1932 –97). A variation on this is that Hamlet is the eponymous hero of *Hamlet* and Jane Eyre the eponymous heroine of Charlotte Brontë's novel.

5. Antonym: a word which is opposite in meaning to another. 'Rich' is an antonym of 'poor', for instance. Other pairs of antonyms include short/tall, dark/light and benevolent/malevolent.

6. Acronym: a word formed from initial letters or graphemes or syllables at the beginning of words. For example, radar originally stood for RAdio Detecting And Ranging. Ofsted comes from OFfice for STandards in EDucation. Oxfam was the OXford fund for FAMine Relief.

7. Metonym: a noun which is used in metonymy – or the use of one simple word to stand for a much larger whole. For example, by referring to alcoholic drink as 'the bottle' or all judges as 'the bench' or using 'the crown' to mean the whole monarchical system. In this context 'bottle', 'bench' and 'crown' are metonyms.

8. Cryptonym: a secret name or word or a code name or word. It is a name given to something or someone which will only be recognised by those in the secret. For example, during the Second World War D-day was the cryptogram for the planned landing on the beaches of Normandy to liberate the French from German occupation.

>> Task 9.10

These, obviously, are just examples. Pupils will have their own ideas.

1. A shark's anterior dorsal fins are on the back of its body towards the front.

2. Anti-social behaviour in our town includes graffiti, vandalism and far too much litter.

3. If you have an old car you have to put antifreeze in the radiator each winter to stop the water freezing.

4. In the line of ten the dance teacher told me to stand in the eighth, or antepenultimate, place.

5. We waited in the anteroom before going into the head's office which opens off it.

6. A group of anti-nuclear demonstrators was protesting at the site of the proposed new power station.

7. Fleming's discovery of the power of penicillin antedated the development of antibiotics by more than ten years.

8. In antebellum Britain Neville Chamberlain tried to prevent war by negotiating with Hitler.

Nuts and bolts

And so to the art of summary – in my opinion one of the most useful (cross-curricular) skills we can equip pupils with. The pointers on page 181 are meant to be a brief how-to guide with practical tips and a clear (I hope) example. Emphasise that the summary, when complete, should be in good flowing English. It shouldn't sound tortured.

But, of course, what pupils really need is plenty of practice which is what Task 9.12 offers. Get pupils to summarise regularly as an exercise until they get the hang of it. It is, after all, only a knack.

>> Task 9.12

A good answer might look something like this – but of course there's no set or 'right' way of doing this.

- In childhood the author noticed that all earthworms have segments and a saddle and her grandfather explained their garden role. Later, as a 16-year-old A level zoology student, she dissected one and learned a great deal more. (42 words)

Additional passage

Bill Bryson, American Anglophile who has lived in the UK for most of the last 30 years and has a whole string of best sellers to his name, writes beautifully about pretty well anything. His trick is to combine insouciance and wit with serious facts and thoughts. He is an extraordinary communicator. It is amazing that I haven't yet included anything by Bryson in any of my English textbooks so it is time to rectify that.

Here he is, discovering things about fossils.

It isn't easy to become a fossil. The fate of nearly all living organisms – over 99.9 per cent of them – is to compost down to nothingness. When your spark is gone, every molecule you own will be nibbled off you or sluiced away to be put to use in some other system. That's just the way it is. Even if you make it into the small pool of organisms, the less than 0.1 per cent that don't get devoured, the chances of being fossilized are very small.

In order to become a fossil several things must happen. First you must die in the right place. Only about 15% of rocks can preserve fossils, so it's no good keeling over on a future site of granite. In practical terms the deceased must become buried in sediment where it can leave an impression, like a leaf in wet mud, or decompose without exposure to oxygen, permitting the molecules in its bones and hard parts (and occasionally softer parts) to be replaced by

---

dissolving minerals, creating a petrified copy of the original. Then as the sediments in which the fossil lies are carelessly pressed and folded and pushed about by the earth's processes, the fossil must somehow maintain an identifiable shape. Finally, but above all, after tens of millions, or perhaps hundreds of millions of years hidden away, it must be found and recognized as something worth keeping.

Only about one bone in a million, it is thought, ever becomes fossilized. If that is so, it means that the complete fossil legacy of all the Americans alive today – that's 270 million people with 206 bones each – will only be about fifty bones, one quarter of a complete skeleton. That's not to say, of course, that any of these bones will ever actually be found. Bearing in mind that they can be buried anywhere within an area of slightly over 9.3 million square kilometres, little of which will ever be turned over, much less examined, it would be something of a miracle if they were. Fossils are, in every sense, vanishingly rare. Most of what has lived on earth has left behind no record at all. It has been estimated that less than one species in ten thousand has made it into the fossil record. That in itself is a stunningly infinitesimal proportion. However, if you accept the common estimate that the Earth has produced thirty billion species of creature in its time, and Richard Leakey and Roger Lewin's statement (in *The Sixth Extinction*) that there are 250,000 species of creature in the fossil record, that reduces the proportion to just one in 120,000. Either way, what we possess is the merest sampling of all the life that earth has spawned.

Moreover, the record we do have is hopelessly skewed. Most land animals, of course, don't die in sediments. They drop in the open and are eaten or left to rot or weather down to nothing. The fossil record, therefore, is almost absurdly biased in favour of marine creatures. About 95 per cent of the fossils we possess are of animals that once lived under water, mostly in shallow seas.

From *A Short History of Nearly Everything* by Bill Bryson (Doubleday, 2003).

Discussion or comprehension points could include:

- thrust of Bryson's argument

- informal tone – use of the second person and expressions, such as 'keeling over'

- sentence length

- changing tone – perhaps becoming more serious and less informal – as the passage proceeds

- presentation of statistics

- success of the piece (or lack of it) as a piece of communication.

Now here's a subject which is full of potential if ever there was one. Fiction is full of men – and sometimes women – who are truly evil and villainous. And, rather more sadly and seriously, there is no shortage in non-fiction either.

If you want more examples, *The Oxford Book of Villains* (1992) edited by the late-lamented John Mortimer has lots to choose from.

Meanwhile, although most of the 'subtle, false and treacherous' figures in fact and fiction have been male it would be good to balance it with a few female examples because, of course, evil behaviour is not entirely a male prerogative. Look at Lady Macbeth, for instance, or Regan and Goneril in *King Lear*. Some of the 'lowlife' and women in Dickens are pretty amoral, too. Take Mrs Bumble and Mrs Claypole in *Oliver Twist*, for example or, from a different social class, the odious Miss Murdstone in *David Copperfield*. And don't forget Jezebel in the Bible (2 Kings) or the archetypical evil female Cruella De Vil from Dodie Smith's *A Hundred and One Dalmatians* (1956).

And as for non-fiction, 'bloody' Mary Tudor is worth looking at along with several of the Borgia women and Catherine de Medici. Or in more recent times – and therefore more chillingly – there are Myra Hindley and Rosemary West who can be researched in online newspaper archives or books.

Another interesting discussion point relevant to this subject is whether anyone in real life – or plausible fiction – is ever totally evil. Are we not all some shade of pale, dark or middling grey rather than black or white? Surely, even the most subtle, false and treacherous villain has one or two redeeming features? Perhaps he (or she) is kind to his mother or his cat. Remember Bill Sykes in Oliver Twist? At the last, relentlessly evil as he is, he cannot bring himself to kill his dog Bullseye – which costs him dearly. Cruella De Vil, on the other hand, is almost a cartoon character (even before Disney got hold of her) because she is painted one hundred per cent a villainess.

>> Task 10.1

1. These seem to me to be the main deducible story elements:

    - eighteenth century barber, Benjamin Barker, lives contentedly in London with wife, Lucy, and baby, Johanna, in a house owned by Mrs Lovett.

    - Judge Turpin wants sex with Lucy – so corruptly gets Barker deported to Australia for 15 years.

    - During his exile, Lucy kills herself and Johanna grows up.

    - Back in London, Barker takes a new name, Sweeney Todd.

    - Todd is very angry and bent on revenge, not least because Turpin is now lusting after Johanna.

    - Mrs Lovett, who dreams of a future with Todd, has kept his razors safely.

    - As 'the demon barber of Fleet Street,' Todd uses the razors to get his revenge.

2. She liked:

- Tim Burton's 'visual flair' which includes a lot of spectacular blood

- the film's macabre humour

- Burton's decision to use actors rather than singers so that the drama is emphasised

- the integration of shortish songs into the drama rather than stopping the action for chorus work

- Johnny Depp's acting and his surprisingly good singing voice

- Helena Bonham Carter's performance as Mrs Lovett and Alan Rickman's as Judge Turpin

- visual effects created by Dante Ferretti and Dariusz Wolski to recreate eighteenth century London graphically (lines 60–64)

- dramatic contrast between the near black and white colouring with the blood

- Colleen Atwood's costumes.

3. She warns the reader that this is a film with a great deal of blood in it '... the literal explosions of arterial blood from slashed throats is truly disturbing and often alarmingly comic'. And she uses words such as 'ghoulishly', 'gothic' and 'fiendish'. She points out that is it a 'terrible and bloody tale' of 'serial murder and corruption' with 'blackest gallows humour' and she uses the word 'macabre' twice. The film 'will not be to everyone's taste', she writes.

4. There is no way that I can even suggest an answer to this. It really is something for each pupil to think about and respond to personally. But there is one point I would raise with the class in discussion:

- This review is over 900 words long – twice the usual length for a newspaper review of this sort. It is very detailed. Is it possible that it tells the reader too much about the film? It details almost all the plot and mentions nearly every aspect of production. Could this review actually deter you from seeing the film because you feel that you now know all about it anyway?

And that, of course, could lead you into a useful discussion about the purpose of reviews and how they should be written. The first option in Personal writing on page 204 offers pupils the opportunity to practise film review writing but, of course, you don't have to insist that they use Passage A as a model if you deem it inappropriate.

>> Task 10.2

1. These are the main points I would look for in a summary:

    - A group of people had voiced objections to some of the policies of Hitler's National Socialist government.

    - In the early hours of 30 June Hitler gave orders – almost unilaterally ('I had very few men with me' – lines 18–19) – that 'the attack' be suppressed with 'an iron fist' (line 12) in Munich, Berlin and Prussia.

    - He gave orders to Goering in Berlin and Prussia that there be a 'purge'.

    - Hitler went to Munich himself.

    - The orders were that 'if any of the mutineers should attempt to resist arrest they were immediately to be struck down with armed force' (lines 39/34) – that is killed – because Hitler is not now 'prepared to exercise clemency' (line 27). He effectively pronounces the death penalty for each of the 'mutineers' by saying that 'certain death is his lot'.

    - 'I gave the order to shoot' (line 36). The 'traitors' were, by implication, stormed and shot in their homes or meeting places.

2. Hitler argues that:

    - he is responsible for the security of Germany

    - the 'fate of the German people' (line 32) depends on their not being threatened by 'mutinous divisions' (line 33)

    - when the problem is urgent – 'the necessity for acting with lightning speed' – a quick decision has to be made by the person in charge

    - Germany has been weak in the past. Now it must 'find the strength to destroy such creatures' (line 63)

    - at times of national emergency like this it is right for him to become 'the supreme justicar of Germany' (line 32).

3. Hitler shows his ruthlessness:

    - in his frequent use of highly emotive language to describe the protestors and their views: '... burn out down to the raw flesh the ulcers of this poisoning of the wells of our domestic life' (lines 37–38) – note the glaring mixed metaphor, too – 'breaks loyalty, breaks faith, breaks sacred pledges'

    - in the dismissive nouns and noun phrases by which he refers to the objectors: 'mutineers', 'conspirators', 'traitors', 'offenders', 'ringleaders', 'such creatures', 'little culprits', 'great criminals', 'agitators', 'destroyers', poisoners of the wellspring of German public opinion

    - by having killed without trial anyone who disagrees with or opposes him. The word 'decimation' (line 33) is particularly chilling.

4. He stresses:

   - that he is acting to protect Germany: 'A nation must know that its existence – and that is guaranteed through its internal order and security – can be threatened by no one with impunity' (lines 40–41)

   - that traitors must be 'the first sacrifice' because anyone who 'rises against Germany' has to be punished immediately because of the consequences of his act

   - that Germany is his prime, single-minded concern. 'I have only to see to it that Germany's lot should not be intolerable'.

   Note also Hitler's:

   - apparent honesty: by speaking very plainly – 'I gave the order to shoot' – he gives the impression that he is telling the truth and not hiding anything

   - rhetorical skill: dismissing the protestors so emotively and praising Germany and Germans so often (seven times) he is probably taking his listeners with him. Skilful use of repetition ('breaks' in lines 69–70, for instance) helps, too

   - decisiveness: which is usually approved of in national leaders.

Additional discussion point

Passage B is a translation and in places the English is very awkward and clumsy. Look, for instance, at the sentence beginning 'The nation …' in line 40. Or the one beginning 'He who …' in line 66. Ask pupils how these could be improved.

Do pupils think that Hitler used language clumsily or is the translation weak? Bear in mind that German often uses longer sentences than English and that there are specific rules about word order which do not apply in English.

If the translator had used better, more incisive English would we have lost the sense of Hitler's Germanic voice and style?

>> Task 10.3

1. Stanley was expected to:

   - make easy sources of wealth taken from Africa – especially ivory – available to King Leopold.

   To this end he had to:

   - set up a trading base on the coast ('near the river's mouth')

   - build a road parallel with the main 1,000 mile navigable Congo. This had to circumvent rapids in a mountainous area

- hire porters to carry sections of steamboat along the road towards the interior

- have the steamboats rebuilt upriver so that he and his men could penetrate deeper into the country

- establish a series of trading stations along the river

- write a book about his experiences to be vetted by Leopold.

2. Leopold:

- concealed his involvement by working through the Committee for Studies of the Upper Congo

- disguised the project as education through the name of this committee and statements to the press: 'Only scientific explorations are intended' (line 61)

- personally owned a large block of shares in the committee but got a Belgian banker to manage them for him so that their true ownership was not obvious

- made sure that one of his closest aides, Colonel Maximilien Strauch presided over the committee

- insisted that Stanley and his European staff signed what would now be called 'gagging agreements'

- often primly argued that there was a clause in the committee's charter which forbade it from working for political gain

- reserved the right to control the content of Stanley's intended book.

3. A good answer might go something like this:

- Hochschild is, by implication, very condemnatory of Stanley and of Leopold's activities. He writes, for example, 'Of the riches Leopold hoped to find in the Congo' (line 20), which doesn't pretend that the Belgian King had any intention other than to exploit the country for money. In the same sentence, he suggests that Leopold is like a greedy child or manic adult for whom ivory 'gleamed most brightly in his imagination'. Later, in line 58, he overtly states that Leopold was doing one thing but saying another, pegged on the emotive and damning word 'ambitious'.

- Stanley, on the other hand, is an employee who has to work round Leopold's ambitions but he is 'savvy', a word with rather unattractive connotations of cunning and self-interest in this context. Hochschild points out that Stanley insisted on payment in advance which shows that he didn't trust Leopold or the Belgian organisations he hid behind. This is, Hochschild implies, a man who will do anything for money.

- Hochschild also criticises Stanley for hiring deliberately two inexperienced Englishman apparently just so he could complain about their lack of knowledge and understanding. They are 'in the tradition of Stanley's inept subordinates' (line 44), which is Hochschild's way of saying that Stanley, perhaps for some reason of personal inadequacy, had a habit of taking on useless staff.

>> Task 10.4

You could write a very full and detailed essay about this passage, which is laden with sub-text, so I would encourage pupils to look at it very closely, bringing out some of these points, although this is not – as it can never be – an exhaustive list:

- Heathcliff, who enters in 'an interval of silence', is, at least initially, disinclined to small talk or offering his visitor a welcome.

- He is assertively violent with the dogs ('a punch of his foot') and with his servant Joseph, although Joseph does not come when he's called so, by implication, he is not cowed by Heathcliff. Neither, perhaps, is the 'lusty dame' who comes from the kitchen to sort out the dogs. This heightens the sense of mystery about Heathcliff. What do these people know which Lockwood does not?

- He seems determined to show Lockwood that he is not prepared to put himself out or hurry to help him ('I don't think they moved one second faster than usual').

- He is rude, implying that Lockwood, a visitor, has behaved inappropriately in his, Heathcliff's, house: 'They won't meddle with persons who touch nothing.' It contravenes all the usual conventions of hospitality, especially in the formal nineteenth century, to say 'What the devil is the matter?' to a visitor, too.

- The aggressive dogs – variously described as 'fiends', 'combatants', 'the whole hive' (as if they were bees), 'ruffianly' and 'a pack of curs' who behave 'wolfishly' and do a lot of growling such as the 'long guttural snarl'. The first time Heathcliff speaks (line 15) he growls as if he were one of the dogs. This has the effect of momentarily dehumanising him.

- The dogs, like 'the herd of possessed swine' (a reference to Jesus's casting of devils into a herd of pigs, Matthew, Chapter 8, verse 32), or a 'brood of tigers', are untrustworthy in Lockwood's eyes. If Heathcliff is like his dogs then he, too, is not to be trusted.

- Yet, Heathcliff clearly knows how to behave when he wants to be charming: 'Take a glass of wine?' and 'Your health, sir'. He also, when he's ready, chats in a more relaxed manner to Lockwood about the house he's living in: 'a discourse on the advantages and disadvantages of my present place of retirement.' Lockwood, rather patronisingly, finds him 'intelligent'. This must mean that Emily Brontë wants us to know that Heathcliff chooses to behave outrageously, when he does, for reasons of his own.

- Heathcliff, when his 'countenance relaxed into a grin', is laughing at the pompous, self-important Lockwood, who cannot see the funny side of this situation himself and does not want 'to yield the fellow further amusement at my expense'.

- Heathcliff makes it clear that he does not want Lockwood to visit again ('evidently wished no repetition of my intrusion'), although Lockwood, tiresomely and oddly, decides that the next day he will 'go, notwithstanding', which has the effect of making the reader look past and through the narrator to sympathise with Heathcliff.

>> Task 10.5

1. The 'blunderbuss' is the porter in the house which is so large it has more than 345 chimneys – hence the need for a porter. He uses the blunderbuss, a primitive gun, to defend himself or threaten potential intruders.

   The 'truncheon' (and Tom meets two different ones in this passage) is a policeman. The truncheon, a short, slender club with a handle at one end, was the control weapon with which all British policeman were traditionally equipped (and still are, although they now have other devices too) from the founding of the Metropolitan Police in 1829.

   Whether or not you find these metonyms effective (or irritating) is probably a matter of personal taste. It is, however, worth pointing out to pupils that metonymy here enables the writer to:

   - make it clear that Tom sees the blunderbuss and the truncheon before he is aware of a human being. It is childlike and appealing

   - depersonalise these men by referring to them as 'it' rather than 'he' and there is no question of their having names.

2. This passage is clearly intended to be witty or at least ironic, although one's response to it is personal. For example:

   - The 'prison-lists' at line 17 are a way of referring to the huge number of people working in the house. It is as if they were in prison and are commenting on working conditions.

   - Tom's childish hyperbole in thinking the walls are 'at least ninety miles high' is gently funny.

   - The huge house has at least 345 chimneys – excessive by any standards and especially at a time when many poor city dwellers are living dozens to a room in tenement blocks. Although this isn't inherently funny it is wryly laughable because it's ridiculous.

   - Mr Grimes is, at this moment, a comic figure, wedged in a chimney unable to free his arms.

   - The metonyms are funny (see above).

   - The comparison of the truncheon with Mr Punch in a Punch and Judy show whacking Grimes on the head is meant to be amusing in a slapstick way.

   - Kingsley means us to smile at the bully Grimes being unable to defend himself or light his pipe.

   - There is a mild, humorous side-swipe at policemen in general and their ineptitude in the last paragraph. The 'well-trained' (or not) policeman is, by implication, only ready to 'avenge any transgression against morality of order' because Grimes is a sitting target.

3.   The two passages are very different because:

- Passage D is much lighter in tone than Passage C.

- Passage D has an overt didactic purpose – to alert readers to the everyday horrors of the work poor people (especially children) have to do.

- Passage C is much more mysterious than Passage D.

- Passage D is a third person narrative while Passage C is written in diary form so there's a lot more personal feeling and emotive language in Passage C.

- Passage C seems to have a remote, timeless rural setting unlike everyday life as most people know it. Passage D is about ordinary people at work and feels much more down to earth.

- The language in Passage C is denser and more intense ('prudential considerations' and 'no intimation of ascending') than that of Passage D – partly to characterise the narrator.

- A child is at the heart of Passage D and we see events from his point of view although the story is told by an omniscient author. In Passage D, the central figures are all adults. The simpler language of Passage D is part of Kingsley's establishing of Tom as a child protagonist.

On the other hand they are similar in that both:

- were written in the mid-nineteenth century, separated by only 15 years

- use humour enjoyed by some characters but by-passing others. Grimes being stuck in the chimney 'just like Punch' and Lockwood's being left to fend off 'Half-a-dozen four-footed fiends' with a poker are both examples of situation comedy.

But let pupils work out for themselves what effect these other considerations have on their preferences.

>> Task 10.6

As they near the end of Year 9 with GCSE (or IGCSE) and sixth form work not that far ahead, some pupils, at least, will be ready to tackle a full-scale traditional literary criticism essay. And 'Porphyria's Lover' is a good poem for this because it's dramatic but reasonably accessible and straightforward with plenty of meaty things to write about. Here are some points, in no particular order, to nudge them towards during preparatory discussion:

- The use of the weather at the beginning to set the scene. The 'sullen wind' with its 'spite' and determination to 'vex the lake' prefigures some of what the narrator is feeling. John Ruskin's term 'pathetic fallacy' may help.

- The chilling effect of choosing the lover as narrator and reinforcing it by calling the poem 'Porphyria's Lover' rather than, say 'Porphyria's Death'. He doesn't justify the murder because to him it is a perfectly reasonable thing to do to establish ultimate possession and stop things changing now that he knows 'Porphyria worshipped me'. He asserts that she is 'mine, mine, fair' and he kills her quite casually: 'I found/A thing to do', and 'And strangled her'. It might be worth comparing the poem, if you have time, with Browning's 'The Last Duchess', also about a man who kills a woman (or has her killed) rationally and ruthlessly.

- 'Soiled gloves' (line 12): a symbol of lost virginity and her vulnerable status (in the nineteenth century) as a trusting, giving, unmarried woman rather than a wife. In some ways, the lover treats her like a prostitute but she clearly is not. She tells him she loves him (line 21) and this is evidently, from the accustomed way she attends to the fire in the cottage, not the first time the pair has met like this. She trusts him enough to 'put my arm about her waist' and make 'her smooth shoulder bare'.

- The lilting, sinister rhyme scheme which, although the 60-line, very carefully patterned poem is written without stanza divisions divides it into five line sections rhyming ABABB/CDCDD/ and so on. The effect of the three B rhymes 'pain', 'again', 'stain' (lines 42, 43 and 44) or 'head', 'fled' and 'instead' lines 52, 53 and 54) is to drive the poem, and our engagement with the narrator's thoughts, forward quickly to their macabre conclusion: 'And thus we sit together now,/And all night long we have not stirred'.

- The plosive and alliterative 'Blushed bright beneath my burning kiss' which almost evokes the sound of his gloating over her and really highlights the horror of his passion and what he has done.

- The comparison of her dead blue eye, which he opens 'warily', with a closed flower bud which holds a bee. It is a strange metaphor because bees do not get trapped in buds. They visit open flowers. And, even if one were trapped, it would buzz out as soon as the bud was opened. Here the narrator seems to be comparing with a bee (furry, yellow, active and noisy) the blue eye which it thinks is laughing again. Presumably this is part of Browning's characterisation of the narrator as an unstable, unfathomable killer?

Additional discussion point

If you feel strong enough to discuss the horror of the necrophilia which lurks beneath 'Porphyria's lover', don't forget the delights of the word itself. From the Greek (*nekros* a corpse and *philos* loving) it literally means loving of the dead. Compare:

necropolis, necrotic, necrolatry

Francophilia, philanthropist, philosopher, bibliophile

Writing about literature and Task 10:7

Here is another example of how pupils might comment on a couple of sentences of prose, this time based on these sentences from Passage A:

But Burton has a soft spot for a certain type of monster. Instead of the gruesome exploits of a pair of avaricious murderers he gives us a very human tragedy of lost love and the devastating consequences of obsessive revenge.

The reviewer opens this short paragraph with a short, simple sentence which acts as an introduction to the ideas she develops in the second sentence. She links it with what has gone before by starting with the conjunction 'but' which gives it a slightly informal tone. Moreover, the first sentence assumes in the reader some knowledge of Burton's other films, which by implication also feature 'a certain type of monster'. In the second, more grammatically complex, sentence she packs in several informative phrases around the subject 'he' and the verb 'gives'. Her adjectives – 'gruesome', 'avaricious', 'devastating' and 'obsessive' are unusually strong and expressive. There is a contrast in the balance of the second sentence, too, hanging on the word 'instead'. We might be expecting a horror story but we get a human tragedy.

>> Task 10.9

Note: Old English (OE in dictionaries) is, of course, the language spoken in England between the final departure of the Romans in the fifth century and the Norman Conquest in 1066 – the so called 'Dark Ages'. I think we have to teach pupils this carefully so that they don't sloppily misuse the term to mean any English which pre-dates what they hear on twenty-first century television.

1. murderer: from Old English *morth* and related to Latin *mors* (death)

2. villain: from Old French *villein*, a serf derived from Latin *villanus*, an estate worker with links to Latin *villa*, a house. Implication is that some impoverished workers turned to crime and eventually the meaning of the word changed. Workers came to be regarded as criminals

3. tyrant: from Greek *turannos*, a tyrant. Compare tyrannosaurus, a tyrannical lizard

4. despot: from Greek *despotes*, lord or master

5. blood: from Old English *blod* and related to Old German word *bluot*

6. homicide: literally the killing of a man from Latin *homo* (man) and *caedere* (to kill). Compare words such as suicide, patricide, regicide.

>> Task 10.10

These suggestions are just examples. Pupils should, as ever, come up with their own.

1. My uncle, a man of eclectic interests, belongs to the Royal Geographical Society, drives an old Mercedes and writes theatre reviews for his local paper.

2. If you have Wi-fi in your home it is a bit perverse to insist on using mobile broadband because it means you are paying twice.

3. 'We're all in this together and anyone who is mutinous will be shot,' declared the pirate from the deck in the spoof play.

4. Difficult and controversial legal cases sometimes lead, eventually, to a disinterested judicial enquiry.

5. Britain is networked with eighteenth and nineteenth century canals which were precursors to the railways.

6. Islam is attracting a growing number of neophytes who, because the culture is new to them, are fascinated by the religious traditions.

7. Suddenly, as midnight struck, there was a plethora of bells and fireworks.

8. Bill Gates, the world's richest man, is also one of its greatest philanthropists having given many millions of dollars to the trusts he has set up and the charities he has founded.

9. I find Tube journeys vexatious when they involve several irritating changes.

10. When a new strain of flu threatens doctors have to be vigilant so that every case is identified and reported.

11. Porphyria's unremorseful lover shows pleasure rather than regret at having killed her.

12. In 2009, many transgressions were revealed in the expenses claims of British Members of Parliament.

13. Despite her best endeavours, my mother cannot persuade my little brother to eat fruit.

14. Can we prevail upon you to join us for supper on Thursday?

15. Saddam Hussein's 'subtle false and treacherous' regime in Iraq attempted to annihilate the Kurds.

>> Task 10.11

- strata, fungi
- theses, automata
- seraphim, criteria
- termini, tempi
- media

>> Task 10.12

- sons-in-law, coats-of-arms
- tablespoonsful, bucketsful
- maids-of-honour, lookers-on
- courts-martial, mothers-in-law

Get it right

I feel passionately about this convention because it is so clear and straightforward. It is a rule and it works. It is a foolproof way of distinguishing parts of books (such as poems) from whole book titles and an easy way of distinguishing titles such as **Hamlet** from references to the eponymous hero, Hamlet.

I have never understood why we – as teachers – persist in teaching young children to pepper their work with inverted commas instead of using the more adult underlining/italics for book titles. It makes it very difficult to get them out of the habit when they arrive at senior or secondary school.

They will have to do it for citations in essays and theses at university so as I tell the pupils in *English Year 9* it makes sense to 'get into good habits now'.

Wide range reading

I am a greedy and eclectic reader – as I want pupils and all users of *English Year 9* to be. Here are a few more titles, examples of my recent reading, to add to the recommended list.

- **Guernica** by Dave Boling (2008), in which the German officer who masterminds the bombing of the city in Northern Spain is presented almost as a personification of evil and amorality. The gripping story – set against a bit of history which isn't visited very often – is about a family and how it was affected by the horrors at Guernica in 1937, as well as featuring Picasso's famous response.

- **The Bride's Farewell** by Meg Rossoff (2009). Written for teenagers, this is the story of a feisty girl in the rural England of the early 1800s. She runs away from home on her wedding morning to avoid being pinned down. On her travels she meets people of all sorts, some decent but others who are subtle, false or treacherous in varying degrees.

- **Bad Company** by Mike Walker (2009) is also aimed at pre-adult readers and is a chillingly plausible adventure story about a south London lad who is sent to his father in Indonesia for the summer. But his father keeps the 'bad company' of the title and Danny ends up on a boat in the Indian Ocean which is also carrying some ruthless men. Then it is attacked by pirates. Quite a page turner and very well written.

- **Running Wild** by Michael Morpurgo (2009) is about, among other things, tiger and orang-utan poaching, also in Indonesia. Will, the narrator, is an English boy on holiday at the time of the tsunami and there's a lot of loss in this compelling story. Mister Anthony takes a lot of beating for villainy.

Additional passage

In Shakespeare's 1604 play Measure for Measure, *Isabella's brother is sentenced to death for getting his girlfriend pregnant. The laws of Vienna, where the play is set, have just been tightened up because everything has become very lax. Sex outside marriage is now a crime punishable by death. So Isabella goes to Angelo, the very strict man temporarily in charge of the city, to plead for her brother's life. The subtle, false and treacherous Angelo then shows himself in his true colours by demanding – to her amazement and anger – Isabella's virginity in exchange for mercy for her brother.*

Make sure pupils read this aloud in (perhaps mixed) pairs, preferably several times and ideally on their feet to act it. This is drama, after all.

ISABELLA : … most pernicious purpose! – Seeming, seeming! –
I will proclaim thee, Angelo; look for 't:
Sign me a present pardon for my brother,
Or with outstretch'd throat I'll tell the world
Aloud what man thou art.

ANGELO: Who will believe thee, Isabel?
My unsoil'd name, th' austereness of my life,
My vouch against you, and my place i' the state,
Will so your accusation overweigh,
That you shall stifle in your own report,
And smell of calumny. I have begun;
And now I give my sensual race the rein:
Fit thy consent to my sharp appetite:
Lay by all nicety and prolixious blushes,
That banish what they sue for; redeem thy brother
By yielding up your body to my will;
Or else he must not only die the death,
But thy unkindness shall his death draw out
By lingering sufferance. Answer me tomorrow,
Or, by the affection that now guides me most,
I'll prove a tyrant to him. As for you,
Say what you can, my false o'erweighs your true.

From *Measure for Measure* by William Shakespeare (1604): Act II, scene 4, lines 150–170.

Discussion or comprehension points could include:

● Isabella's threat

● Angelo's response to her threat

● his tyrannical declaration that if she doesn't give him what he wants, Angelo will have the brother tortured before death

● 'my false o'erweighs your true' as a summary of the situation

● vocabulary Angelo uses to describe his lust – 'sensual race', 'sharp appetite', 'affection', etc.

● assuming that pupils don't know the play, what is Isabella likely to say next?